To Carleen
Happy Birthday
8/2/91   *Love*
DAD & GRACE

Kinsale
Good Food
Circle

Recipes from Ireland's Gourmet Capital

Foreword by Hugh Leonard

Compiled and Edited by Roz Crowley

FORUM PUBLICATIONS

Acknowledgements:

Drawings and Cover Design: Frank Sanquest

Book Design: Roz Crowley

Cover: 'A Breakfast' by Frans Snyders.
Reproduced by kind permission of
The National Gallery of Ireland.

Publishers: Forum Publications, Currabaha, Cloghroe,
Blarney, Co. Cork. Ireland.

ISBN: 0 9510018 1 7

Printed by: Litho Press, Midleton, Co. Cork

Foreword

The following sounds like an example of the 'Higher Truth' (euphemism for a brazen lie), but it happened in Kinsale perhaps eight years ago: We dined so well at the Vintage that we reserved the same table for the following evening and as we entered Actons Hotel at a late hour, I asked the night porter if a night-cap was a possibility. 'To be sure it is sir' he replied. Then, as we passed through the port-holes, he added: 'would you like a drink while you are waiting?'

Somehow the incident sums up the mild dottiness which infuses that most beguiling of all Irish towns, one to which I return with reluctance, for the knowledge is there that each visit carries with it the pain of a leavetaking and, in telling the story, I find that I indict myself. In Kinsale, it verges on sinfulness to resist in succession any restaurant no matter how fine. You do not have to go to France to understand the meaning of *embarasse de richesse*. The miracle of Kinsale lies not in the wealth and variety of its good restaurants but that the greatest of Irish weaknesses has been overcome. I mean lack of stamina. I once said, and was rebuked by the columnists, that in Ireland nothing lasts except the grudges. I stick to my guns; campaigns to combat illegal parking and wage war on litterbugs start off with tremendous zest and fury; then the momentum dies and we all park on double yellow lines again and throw sweet papers out of the car window. My own town Dalkey actually rivalled Kinsale for a while with six restaurants that were first-class. Now there are but two (my opinion).

By relentless vigilance Kinsale has not only attained a high standard but maintained it down the years. This book is its monument and its gloat. I shall not reflect upon the gross unfairness that so many superlative meals should be found within so small a space, much to the impoverishment of the great elsewhere. I do take it amiss, however, that Roz Crowley should, for the purpose of having these words written, have sent this book to one who is undergoing the privations of a five-week diet.

Hugh Leonard

History of Kinsale

Kinsale, on the sea in the shelter of its hillsides is situated 19 miles from Cork City in Southern Ireland. The picturesque town has been in existence since before records began. To and from Kinsale's sheltered harbour ships sailed trading with the great powers of the Roman world carrying cargoes of great riches. Also came ships using the shelter of the harbour to escape their enemies and the inclement elements of sea storms.

Its first known Charter dates back to 1334 but the town's first formal beginnings are thought to go back to the Normans in 1177. They set up the original walled town near the harbour which in time extended as trade flourished.

In 1200 the original St. Mulrose church, which is one of the few Medieval churches still in use in Ireland, was built. Kinsale also had its medieval guilds at that time and examples of the works of Goldsmiths and Silversmiths of the era still survived. In the 16th century Desmond Castle was used to hold Frenchmen during the napoleonic Wars.

Between December 1601 and January 1602 the siege and ultimately the Battle of Kinsale took place north of the town. The Spanish fleet held the bay and the town awaiting the arrival of the great O'Neill and O'Donnell who were marching with their forces from the north of the country. However by January 2nd 1602 the English under Mountjoy had gained victory. This battle is considered to be a turning point in European History,

Long famed in battle the magnificent old fortresses of James and Charles Fort both built in the 17th century are still preserved to this day and it is quite easy to imagine the hustle and bustle of the great armies which occupied them.

Bringing us more into the present the town was the scene of the inquest on the victims of the Lusitania which was a casualty of World War I. The verdict was given world wide publicity. In 1966 Kinsale was awarded the flag of the Council of Europe.

Today the reputation of Kinsale as the Gourmet Capital of Ireland is totally accepted and, as we stand poised on the brink of a united European Community, perhaps we should look to Kinsale as small piece of the Island which has always been European in its outlook

ACTONS HOTEL: This Grade A hotel is a characterful period building originally owned by Sidney Acton whose grandfather had many businesses in Kinsale since the mid-19th century. Now a Trusthouse Forte hotel, Actons offers table d'hote and à la carte menus in its Captain's Table restaurant. Sunday lunch with Jazz as well as full hotel facilities.including indoor swimming pool are features. The recipes in this book give a flavour of what's on offer from the kitchen.

BERNARDS: In the old market area of Kinsale Bernard and his wife Angela run this small 28-seat restaurant. Very much belonging to the old school Bernard trained under the guidance of the Gaio brothers and their influence can be seen on the menu. In his selection of recipes for this book Bernard has chosen the more unusual dishes on his menu, using rabbit, smoked chicken and fish which are always available fresh in Kinsale.

BISTRO: Carole Norman and Miles Cattell have converted a unique 150-year old building into a bistro of friendly and informal atmosphere. This is a place to eat or drink as little or as much as you wish. They specialize in fish cooked as simply as possible with lobster and crab available nightly, plainly served with a varied salad platter and potatoes of the day. Vegetarians and meat-eaters are also well catered for. The recipes in this book show Carole and Miles' versatility and style.

BLUE HAVEN: Brian and Ann Cronin's hotel and restaurant is situated in the heart of Kinsale on the site of the old fish market. The garden restuarant, overlooking the floodlit garden, offers à la carte and gourmet dinner menus with an emphasis on shellfish and seafood. The smaller Quay Room restaurant offers more informal dining with bar food available in the Haven Bar, conservatory and patio. The recipes in this book show Brian and Ann's enthusiasm for the use of locally picked wild spinach and locally farmed mussels which are features of their menus.

COTTAGE LOFT: Located in the centre of Kinsale on Main Street, Michael & Carolanne's 100-year old townhouse has its restaurant on the ground floor with bed and breakfast accomodation overhead. The interior has an old world charm, decorated in rich deep tones giving a very warm and welcoming ambience. Some of their better known recipes using seafood are featured in this book along with their game, meat and vegetarian recipes which are available on the à la carte and table d'hote menus.

IL RISTORANTE: Situated just outside Kinsale at the foot of James' Fort, Roberto Pons and his Cork wife Celine have established Kinsale's only Italian restaurant. Roberto comes from Bordighera on the Italian Riviera where his family had a restaurant for many years. The building was originally two fisherman's cottages and its elegant dining room overlooks the Bandon estuary. Roberto & Celine serve high quality Italian food with emphasis on a high standard of service with a carefully chosen wine list featuring quality Italian vintages..

5

JIM EDWARDS:: This fully licensed restaurant owned by Jim & Paula Edwards is located on Market Quay in Kinsale. This restaurant began life as a pub and slowly food became a popular feature. The dining room here is spacious and set out on three different levels with a nautical theme throughout. With fresh fish on the doorstep daily and a lobster tank in the restaurant, it follows that the menu has a large variety of seafood. The recipes given in this book show that meat and poultry feature well too.

MAN FRIDAY: Situated high up on Scilly, owner-chef Philip Horgan and his wife Joss run a fully licenced restaurant which is entered through a cave-like tunnel. Inside, the log cabin feeling is enhanced by the warm, cosy interior of stone walls and pine panelling. This is one of the oldest restaurants in Kinsale. The style of the food is progressive with a French flair with some old favourites which appear in this book. Friendly service in a relaxed atmosphere is one of its hallmarks.

MAX'S WINE BAR: Max was owner Wendy Tisdall's tall dark and handsome Doberman who guarded Kinsale's first wine bar 14 years ago. An open peat fire burns in a large stone fireplace and polished antique tables gleam in the candlelight. Max's is about food and drink, meetings and reunions, incident, camaraderie and the warmth and friendliness of the staff. The recipes chosen for this book have a view to speed of assembly with all the style of haute cuisine.

TRIDENT HOTEL: A waterfront hotel the Trident has 40 bedrooms and a spectacular view of Kinsale harbour. The Savannah Restaurant has à la Carte and Table d'hote menus while the Fisherman's Wharf bar offers a bar food menu from simple snacks to seafood and steak dishes. The South Coast Carvery operates for Sunday lunch, offering a choice of meats carved to customers' liking. The recipes in this book are taken from the Savannah Restaurant menus.

VINTAGE: This small, cosy and romantic restraurant is to be found on Main Street in Kinsale. There is an open fire in the dining room, two-hundred-year old beams and the original masts from sailing ships which came into Kinsale. Owner/chef Michael Riese who was formerly chef at the Four Seasons in his native Hamburg along with his wife Marie like to conjure up a menu remarkable for its freshness of ingredients and approach which can be seen here in this book.

WHITE HOUSE: The oldest licensed premises in Kinsale this centrally-located building has been a familiar landmark to generations of local people and is something of an institution in the town. Dinner menus, bar menus and tourist menus are on offer with the chef's fillet steak heavily featured and is included in this book. Proprietors Michael and Rose Frawley endeavor to mix relaxation with good food, with pre-dinner and post-dinner drinks available in the lounge bar.

Some useful recipes and explanations

Al Dente:
Firm to bite. Cooked until the crispness is gone but not soft.

Bain Marie:
A flat open vessel, half-filled with water, which is kept at a temperature just below boiling point; used to keep sauces, soups etc. hot without further cooking. The term can also mean a baking tin half-filled with water in which baked custards, mousses and other egg dishes stand whilst cooking, to prevent over-heating

Béarnaise Sauce:
Place 4 tablespoons of wine or tarragon vinegar, 1 skinned and chopped shallot and a few sprigs of tarragon in a small saucepan over a gentle heat and reduce to about 1 tablespoon. Stir this into 2 egg yolks in a basin and cook over a pan of simmering water until slightly thickened. Whisk in 3 oz of butter a little at a time, then season to taste.

Beurre Blanc:
Peel and chop six shallots. Place in a saucepan with a $1/4$ litre (8 fl. oz.) wine vinegar, $1/3$ litre (11 fl. oz.) fish stock and ground pepper. Reduce by two-thirds. Cut 250g (8 oz.) butter into cubes. Remove the saucepan from the heat and add the butter all at once, beating by hand until smooth. Season with salt and pepper and pour into a warmed sauceboat to serve. Keep warm in a bain-marie until required.

Blanching:
Treating food with boiling water in order to whiten it, preserve its natural colour, loosen the skin or remove a flavour which is too strong. Two ways of blanching are
(1) To plunge the food into boiling water; use this method for skinning tomatoes.
(2) To bring it to the boil in the water; used to whiten veal and sweet berries or to reduce the saltiness of kippers and pickled meat.

Chantilly Cream:
Fresh cream beaten to the consistency of a mousse, sweetened, and flavoured with vanilla or other flavours.

Clarifying Butter:
Melt some butter in a heavy saucepan; do not stir. Remove the scum with a spoon then carefully pour the butter into another container so that the whitish sediment stays in the pan - this is discarded and the sediment-free butter is used in many sauces and for frying.

Demi - Glace:
Boil down to reduce by two-thirds a mixture of 17 fl oz espagnole sauce (see below) and $1^1/3$ pints of clear brown stock. Remove from the heat, add 3 tablespoons Madeira, and strain. A handful of sliced mushroom stalks may be added during cooking.

Espagnole Sauce:
Fry 1 oz streaky bacon in 1 oz butter for 2-3 minutes. Add 1 shallot, skinned and chopped, 1 oz mushroom stalks, washed and chopped and 1 small carrot, peeled and chopped and fry for a further 3-5 minutes, or until lightly browned. Stir in 2-3 level tablespoons flour and stir until it turns brown. Remove from the heat and gradually add $1/2$ pint beef stock, stirring. Return the pan to the heat and stir until stock, thickens; add a bouquet garni (bunch of herbs), 2 level tablespoons tomato paste and salt & pepper. Reduce the heat and allow to simmer for 1 hour. Strain, re-heat and skim off any fat. Re-season if necessary.

Fish Stock:
Clean a cod's head or wash fish trimmings and use bones of white fish. Put in a saucepan, cover with water, add some salt, bring to the boil and skim. Reduce the heat and add a little bouquet garni and a thinly sliced onion - a little lemon juice and a glass of dry white wine are optional. Cover and simmer for at least $1/2$ hour.

Julienne:
Fine strips of vegetables.

Reducing:
The process of boiling a liquid in an uncovered pan, in order to evaporate surplus liquid and give a more concentrated result.

Roux:
A mixture of equal amounts of fat and plain flour cooked together to form the basis for sauce and for thickening sauces and stews.

Sweating:
Cooking a food (usually a vegetable) very gently in melted fat until it exudes juices.

CONVERSION TABLES – WEIGHT

1. Exact equivalents
(to two places of decimals)

Metric	British
25g	0.88 oz
100g	3.53 oz
1 Kg	2.20 lb

British	Metric
1 oz	28.35g
8 oz	226.78g
1 lb	0.45 Kg (453.6g)
$1^1/_2$ lb	0.68 Kg (680.40g)
2 lb	0.91 Kg (907.2g)

2. Approximate equivalents

Metric	British
25g	1 oz
50g	$1^3/_4$-2 oz
75g	$2^1/_2$ oz
100g	$3^1/_2$ oz
200g	7oz
500g (0.5 Kg)	1 lb 2 oz (18 oz)
1000g (1 Kg)	$2^1/_2$ lb (36 oz)

CONVERSION TABLES – LIQUID MEASURES

1. Exact equivalents (to two places of decimals)

Metric	British
250 ml (0.25 Litre)	0.44 pints
500 ml (0.50 litre)	0.88 pints
1 litre	1.76 pints
British	Metric
1/2 pint	0.28 litres
1 pint	0.57 litres

2. Approximate equivalents

Metric	British
150 ml	1/4 pint
250 ml	scant half pint
300 ml	$^1/_2$pint
500 ml (0.5 litres)	scant pint
750 ml	$1^1/_4$ pints
1000 ml (1 litre)	$1^3/_4$ pints
1.5 litres	$2^1/_2$ pints
2 litres	$3^1/_2$ pints

Actons Hotel

Banana Amsterdam
Seafood salad Hawaii

Walnut soup
Devilled cucumber and tomato soup

Braised red cabbage
Stuffed baked potato

Monkfish with black cherries
Scallops Cionn tSáile

Roast lamb with orange and honey sauce
Fillet Steak Blackforest

Orange roulade
Soufflé Milanaise
Prince Regent gâteau

ACTONS HOTEL

Banana Amsterdam

INGREDIENTS:

1 Banana
1 slice of ham
1 slice of cheese
    Squeeze of lemon
    Mustard.

METHOD:

Wrap peeled banana with a little lemon juice over it in a slice of cheese. Put a little mustard on the slice of ham and wrap around the cheese. Place on a greased dish and grill until cheese has melted. Serve on a corn on the cob dish, decorate with parsley.

Seafood Salad Hawaii

INGREDIENTS:

$2^{1}/2$lbs cod
Salted butter
Mayonnaise
Tomato ketchup
1 tin pineapple finely chopped.
$1^{1}/2$ celery sticks finely chopped.
3 oz. mushrooms.sliced.
Seasoning.
Worcestershire sauce.

METHOD:

Place cod in boiling salted water for about 20 minutes. Drain off, cool down and flake (remove all bones) Mix tomato sauce, worcestershire sauce and mayonnaise (approx.$^{1}/2$ pint) together. Mix rest of ingredients with fish and finally add sauce. Place in fridge, cover and leave to cool.

Serve a portion of seafood on shredded lettuce garnished with a wedge of lemon, slice of cucumber and tomato.

Walnut Soup

ACTONS HOTEL

INGREDIENTS:

4 oz. walnuts
1 oz. butter
2 oz. finely chopped onions
2 tbsp. wholemeal flour
$1^1/2$ pts. vegetable stock.
1 bay leaf.
1 small strip lemon rind.
2 walnuts halved.

METHOD:

Immerse walnuts in water and cook for 5 minutes. Drain and purée. Sauté the onions in butter and flour, then add to the stock. Bring to the boil. Add the lemon rind and bay leaf. Simmer for 10 minutes. Add walnut purée, and correct seasoning. Serve with croûtons and garnish with some whole walnuts.

Devilled Cucumber and Tomato Soup

INGREDIENTS:

2 pt.chicken stock
1 oz tomato purée
1 fl. oz. malt vinegar
$1/2$ tsp. Worcestershire sauce
Juice of $1/2$ lemon.
2 fl. oz. sour cream.

METHOD:

Add the stock to the tomato purée. Finely dice the cucumber and bring the soup to the boil. Add the rest of the ingredients to the soup. Simmer for 10 minutes. Correct seasoning.

ACTONS HOTEL

Braised Red Cabbage

INGREDIENTS:

8oz bacon fat
4 oz. sugar
1 lb. diced onions
1 lb. diced apples.
8 lbs. shredded red cabbage.
$^3/_4$pt. of water or stock.
$^1/_2$ pt. red wine.
2 oz. cider vinegar.
   Salt and pepper.

METHOD:

Sauté the onions in fat with sugar. Add the red cabbage and stock.
Simmer until soft. Add the wine, vinegar and seasoning. Stir well.
NOTE:(white or red cabbage may be braised with salt, pork, bacon,
ham, onion, garlic and various herbs and spices.)

Stuffed Baked Potato

INGREDIENTS:

4 large potatoes
3 Rashers.
3 tbsp. grated cheese.
1 tbsp. chopped parsley.
2 tbsp. butter
2 tbsp. cream
   Salt and pepper

METHOD:

Scrub potatoes well. Make an X on each top. Bake on middle shelf in
a moderate oven - 180c, 350f, gas mark 4. for one hour approximately.
Remove from the oven and while they cool slightly prepare the
stuffing. Combine in a bowl rashers fried until crisp and either
chopped or crumbed grated cheese and chopped parsley. Split the
potatoes carefully down the middle. Scoop out the potato and place
into a bowl with other ingredients. Add butter, cream, seasoning and
mix. Place mixture in potato shells. Sprinkle cheese on top and heat
in a hot oven - 200C, 400F Gas mark 6 for 20 minutes approximately or
until golden brown

Monkfish with Black Cherries

ACTONS HOTEL

INGREDIENTS:

2 lbs. Monkfish cubed.
5 tbsp. lemon juice.
Salt and pepper
5 tbsp. oil
$^1/_2$ pt. stock.
1 shot soya sauce
1 tbsp. curry powder
2 tbsp. stoned black cherries.
2 tbsp. cream.
1 tbsp. cornflour.

METHOD:

Heat the oil and fry the cubed fish. Add the lemon juice and stock. Simmer for approximately 6 minutes. Add cornflour mixed with a little water, curry powder and cherries. Allow to thicken. Add cream and serve on a shell platter or fish plate. Serve with a baked potato or rice.

Scallops Cionn-tSáile

INGREDIENTS:

8 medium scallops
$^1/_2$ onion, diced finely
6 sliced mushrooms
2 tomatoes, deseeded and finely diced
1 tsp chopped parsley
1 tsp chopped chives
$^1/_2$ glass brandy
$^1/_2$ glass dry white wine
$^1/_4$ pt. cream.

METHOD:

Quickly sauté the scallops in a hot pan. Flame with the brandy. Add the white wine and bring to the boil. Remove the scallops and add the diced ingredients. Reduce this by half. Add the cream and reduce to a sauce- like consistency. Add the scallops. Serve two scallop shells per person with rice or baked potato.

Fillet Steak Blackforest

ACTONS HOTEL

INGREDIENTS:

One 8 oz. fillet steak.
Salt and pepper
Paprika
Rosemary.
2 tbsp. cream (stiffly whipped)
1 tbsp. cranberries.

MARINADE:

Red wine, oil, onion, carrot, parsley,
rosemary

METHOD:

Place steak in marinade for at least two hours.
Remove steak from marinade and cook on hot grill. Season. Mix the whipped cream and cranberries and keep cold. Place steak on a plate with lettuce and tomato to garnish. Place a tablespoon of cranberry cream on top of steak. Serve with a salad and baked potato.

Roast Lamb with Orange and Honey Sauce

INGREDIENTS:

1 leg of lamb, boned.
  Salt and pepper
  Juice and rind of 2 oranges
$1/4$ tsp. ground ginger
2 tbsp. clear honey
1 tsp. cornflour
$1/4$ pt. chicken stock

METHOD:

Rub the meat with salt, pepper and ginger and place in a hot oven for 20-30 minutes at 400F, Gas 6, 200C.
Place the peel and juice from oranges into a saucepan with honey and ginger, and heat. Mix the cornflour with the stock. Remove meat from oven, remove some of the fat but leave the juices. Brush the meat with some of the orange and honey mixture. Scatter the orange peel over meat. Cook in the oven for a further 25-30 minutes. Add cornflour mixture to the remaining orange juice, place on heat and thicken. Remove lamb from oven and pour the meat juices into the sauce and heat up. Add some more stock.
Serve with vegetables, and roast potatoes.

Orange Roulade

ACTONS HOTEL

INGREDIENTS:

5 eggs
6 oz. castor sugar
1 lemon, juice and rind
1 orange, juice and rind

METHOD:

Whisk the egg yolks, sugar, juices and rind together. Whisk the egg whites and fold into the mixture. Butter a tray lined with greaseproof paper. Place mixture evenly and bake in a medium oven. Remove when cooked and roll immediately onto sugared greaseproof paper. When cold unroll, fill with fresh cream, slice and serve.

Soufflé Milanaise

INGREDIENTS:

6 egg yolks
6 Egg whites
10 oz. castor sugar.
2 lemons juice and rind.
5 leaves of gelatine.
1 pt. cream.

METHOD:

Tie paper around soufflé mould $^1/2$ ins. above the rim. Cream yolks and sugar to ribbon stage*. Add grated lemon rind and strained juices. Whisk well in bain marie. Add melted gelatine. Whisk until cold. Blend in beaten whites carefully. Place in fridge to set.

To serve, remove paper, hand decorate with chantilly cream, almonds fruits and finger biscuits.

*Ribbon stage: When the mixture will hold the shape of trails made with a spoon.

See P. 7 for chantilly cream.

ACTONS HOTEL

Prince Regent Gateau

INGREDIENTS:

(Sponge Mixture)
7 eggs, separated.
5 oz. castor sugar.
  Pinch of salt.
5 oz. self raising flour

(Filling)
^{1}/2 pt. milk.
1 oz. cornflour
2 oz. castor sugar
1 egg yolk
9 oz. butter
2 oz. chocolate
2 oz. cocoa.

(Icing)
7 oz. plain chocolate

METHOD:

Grease and flour 3 baking trays. Whisk egg yolks and salt until thick. Whisk egg whites with half the sugar until stiff. Whisk in remaining sugar and fold in yolks. Sieve flour and fold into mixture. Spread mix onto trays. Cook for 5-7 minutes.

Filling: Mix a little milk with cornflour. Heat remaining milk with sugar and pour onto cornflour. Return to heat and bring to the boil. Cream butter until soft and beat into cooled cornflour sauce. Melt chocolate in bain marie. Add to buttercream. Add in cocoa powder and spread over sponge. Place one layer on top of the other, cover top and sides and leave to set.

Melt chocolate and pour over the cake to cover. Decorate to suit occasion.

Bernard's

Stir-fried rabbit with green noodles
Envelope of smoked chicken with Marsala

Parmentier potatoes
Potatoes with cream
Ratatouille

Vegetable lasagna

Fillets of sole with prawns

Smoked Ummera chicken breast with orange & green pepper sauce
Rabbit with cider, tarragon & mushrooms

Lemon chiffon pie

Stir-Fried Rabbit with Green Noodles

BERNARD'S

INGREDIENTS:

¹/₄ rabbit
1 tomato
1 portion green noodles, cooked.
¹/₂ small onion, finely chopped
1 clove garlic, finely chopped
2 tbsp. cream

METHOD:

Cut the rabbit into very small pieces. Place the rabbit, onion, garlic and seasoning in a hot pan. Add tomato and cook quickly. Add noodles and combine with all the ingredients. Add cream and serve immediately.

Envelope of Smoked Chicken and Vegetables

INGREDIENTS:

Smoked chicken, finely cut.
Assorted raw vegetables, finely cut.
Puff pastry rolled out to 6"x 6" (The pastry must be very thin to gain full effect from this dish).
¹/₄ cup of cream
Dash of Marsala (Tio Pepe Sherry would be a suitable substitute)
2 oz. butter.
2 to 3 grapes to garnish.

METHOD:

Combine vegetable and chicken (no seasoning) and place in pastry. Fold pastry into a package. Place on a greased and floured tray and brush with egg wash. Cook for 5 minutes in a hot oven until golden brown. In the meantime, for the sauce, put the Marsala, Cream and a pinch of salt in a small saucepan, bring to the boil and reduce until of sauce consistency. Fold in the butter or, if you prefer, omit the butter for a much lighter sauce. Put sauce on a plate, placing the chicken on top.
'Square' off the grapes and place around in the sauce.

Parmentier Potatoes

BERNARD'S

Wash, peel and re-wash potatoes and cut into $\frac{1}{2}$" dice. Dry thoroughly. Heat some oil in a deep fat fryer or deep saucepan to medium heat. Lower in the potatoes carefully - in a fine-meshed basket is the best way - and allow to cook for about ten minutes. The potatoes should not be brown. Drain and set aside until needed. Sauté a finely diced onion and some de-rinded streaky rashers cut into strips then add the potatoes and toss in the pan until golden. Season with salt and pepper

Potatoes with Cream

INGREDIENTS

Potatoes
Leftover ends of cream and milk
Salt & Black pepper

METHOD

Wash, peel and re-wash potatoes and slice finely. Bring milk/cream to boil and lower heat to a simmer. Add the potatoes and bring back to boiling point. Allow to cook until potatoes are just firm. Remove from saucepan and allow to cool.
To serve: Arrange in oven-proof dish and place in a hot oven until brown.

23

BERNARD'S

Ratatouille

INGREDIENTS:

1lb courgettes diced $^{1}/_{4}$"
6 fresh tomatoes, peeled and diced $^{1}/_{4}$"
3 onions,peeled and finely diced
l red pepper, diced $^{1}/_{4}$"
1 green pepper, diced $^{1}/_{4}$"
6 stalks celery, diced $^{1}/_{4}$"
$^{1}/_{2}$ aubergine, diced $^{1}/_{4}$"
1 dessertspoon tomato purée
1 dessertspoon brown sugar
Pinch mixed herbs
4-6 cloves garlic
Salt & pepper

METHOD:

In a heavy saucepan cook the onions slowly with a large knob of butter or 4 dessertspoons olive oil. When soft, but not brown, add the pepper, celery, herbs, tomatoes, tomato purée and brown sugar and mix well. Next add the courgettes and season with salt & pepper. Place a lid of greaseproof paper on top and simmer very gently for 20 minutes. Add the aubergine and cook for a further 5-10 minutes. Correct seasoning and serve. Served on a bed of spaghetti this dish is an appetizing vegetarian dish.

Vegetable Lasagne

BERNARD'S

INGREDIENTS:

Use a selection of all available vegetables e.g. cauliflower, broccoli, mushrooms, courgettes, onions, carrots, peppers, tomatoes etc.

METHOD:

Cut all vegetables into equal sizes. In a large pan place some cooking oil. Heat the pan and start cooking the hard vegetables first i.e. onions, carrots and peppers. Next add cauliflower, broccoli, mushrooms and courgettes. Add a pinch of paprika with some fresh tomatoes and tomatoe purée. Using the tomatoes in this way will create the sauce necessary to coat the pasta. Correct seasoning with salt and pepper. Using cooked pasta (wholemeal) create a layered effect. A cheese sauce can be layered through for extra flavour and nourishment.

Fillets of Sole with Prawns

BERNARD'S

INGREDIENTS:

1 medium black Dover Sole
4 fresh Prawns (shelled)
$^1/_2$ pt. pouring cream.
$^1/_2$ pt. white wine (medium)
Juice of $^1/_2$ lemon
1 tomato
4 sprigs of parsley or any green herb
2 oz. butter

METHOD:

Get your fish shop to skin and fillet the sole. Place one prawn in each of the sole fillets. Roll up and place in a shallow pan with wine, cream and lemon juice. Place a lid on top and poach for 5 minutes or until cooked. Remove and keep warm. Reduce the cooking liquor by half. Fold in butter. Pour sauce over the fish and garnish with tomato rose and parsley. Serve with boiled potatoes and broccoli.

Smoked Ummera Chicken Breast with Orange and Green Pepper Sauce

BERNARD'S

INGREDIENTS: (per person)

1 breast of chicken
1 orange (juice and zest)
1 dessertspoon brown sugar
1 tsp. green peppercorns (Madagascar)

METHOD:

Slice the chicken at an angle and place on a tray with a little water and cover with tin foil. Place in a warm oven for 10 minutes.

Sauce:
Zest the orange with a potato peeler and cut into fine strips. Cook the orange zest with a little water until water boils dry. Add sugar and peppercorns. When the sugar melts add the orange juice and season with a little salt and pepper. A dash of cream and a little butter are optional additions.

Rabbit with Cider Tarragon and Mushrooms

INGREDIENTS:

1 young rabbit
1 small onion finely chopped
1 pinch tarragon, dried
1 cup of mushrooms, sliced
  Dash of Cider
  Salt and pepper
1 oz. cooking oil
  Butter

METHOD:

Remove all the rabbit from the bone. Cut into bite-size pieces and wash thoroughly. In a very hot pan cook the onion, mushrooms and rabbit in oil. Add cider and tarragon and correct seasoning. Butter and cream are optional.

BERNARD'S

Lemon Chiffon Pie.

INGREDIENTS:

8oz plain flour,sifted
1 egg
2oz castor sugar
5oz butter,chopped
Pinch salt

Filling:
1 pint milk
2oz cornflour,sieved (be precise with this measurement)
4oz castor sugar
4 egg yolks
1 vanilla pod or 1 tablespoon vanilla essence
1 lemon,grated & squeezed

Meringue:
4 egg whites

Syrup made from blending 8oz castor sugar with 7 tablespoons water for 5 minutes

METHOD

Sieve flour and salt and add in cold butter. Rub in to a sandy texture. In a separate bowl beat the egg and sugar. Make a well in the centre of the flour and add this mixture. Mix with a fork until in a ball. DO NOT KNEAD. If you do, it will be too elastic and lose its crumbly texture.. Place on a floured plate and chill in the refrigerator until firm.
Roll out the pastry to fit the tin.
Line a greased and floured 12" baking tin with the pastry and prick with a fork. Line the pastry with greaseproof paper or tinfoil and place uncooked rice or dried beans on top i.e bake blind. Place in a preheated oven at 200C Gas 6 400F for 15 minutes. Remove the foil for the last 5 minutes.
Place 2/3 of milk in a heavy saucepan. Add the vanilla & 2oz of the sugar. In a bowl mix the rest of the milk,cornflour,rest of sugar,egg yolks and whisk thoroughly.
Bring the milk to the boil and add in the cold mixture stirring all the time. When the cornflour taste is gone and the custard is thick enough to stand a spoon in (about 10 mins) add the lemon juice and rind. Cook no further.
To prepare meringue:
Place egg whites in a food mixer. In a separate saucepan place the sugar and water. Bring to boil and keep boiling until bubbles start to slow down. Beat the egg whites until stiff and slowly add in the syrup beating constantly. Beat for a further 10 minutes.
Mix 1/3 of this meringue into the vanilla custard folding gently. Place the custard in the pastry case.
Place the rest of the meringue into a piping bag and pipe immediately on top. Place in a medium/hot oven for 2-3 minutes to brown the meringue. Cool slightly then dredge with icing sugar and serve cool.

Bistro

Mussels in spinach
Avocado, tomato & mozzarella bake

Lettuce & sorrel soup
Smoked chicken & black grape soup

Cucumber salad
Baked potatoes with nutmeg
Leeks with almonds

Salmon en papillote

Spanikapita

Beef & Guinness casserole

Walnut tart
Coffee & whiskey cake

BISTRO

Mussels in Spinach

INGREDIENTS:

8oz. fresh spinach, finely chopped.
1 pt. mussels.
$^1/_2$ pt. cream
1 glass white wine.
  Salt and peppeer
$^1/_2$ onion peeled and finely chopped.
1 oz. butter
4/5 sprigs dill chopped.

METHOD:

Place onions, mussels and white wine in a heavy pan with a lid and steam for approximately 5 minutes until mussels have opened. (Discard any mussels that have not opened). Remove opened ones from shells. Reserve the cooking liquids.

Steam the spinach in a very small amount of water until soft, season and place in serving dish leaving the centre of dish empty and keep warm.

Put cream in a pan and reduce. Add reserved cooking liquids and then dill and butter to thicken sauce. Add the mussels to sauce and pour onto spinach and serve.

Avocado, Tomato and Mozzarella Bake

INGREDIENTS:

2 large ripe avocados
4 oz. mozzarella, grated

TOMATO SAUCE

1 lb. ripe tomatoes, skinned and chopped finely.
1 small onion, finely chopped
1 clove garlic, crushed.
1 tsp. tomato purée
2 tbsp. double cream.
Salt and freshly ground black pepper
  1 dessertspoon freshly chopped basil
  Olive Oil.

METHOD:

Heat 1 tablespoon of olive oil in pan and soften onion and garlic for 5 minutes. Add tomatoes, tomato purée, basil and seasoning. Simmer for 15 minutes with lid on. Remove lid and reduce for 10 minutes. Add double cream. Peel and halve the avocados, remove stones and divide into 4 portions. Cut each half diagonally and place in oven-proof dishes, top with tomato sauce and then sprinkle with grated mozzarella. Bake in hot oven for 10 minutes.

Lettuce and Sorrel Soup

BISTRO

INGREDIENTS:

8oz. lettuce
8oz. sorrel
2 oz. butter
2 large potatoes
2 pts. vegetable stock.
  Salt and pepper
4 tbsp. cream.

METHOD:

Wash sorrel and lettuce and chop roughly. Heat butter in heavy pan and add vegetables. Cook gently for 5 minutes and then add the peeled and finely chopped potatoes. Stir well and then pour on the vegetable stock. Add seasoning and simmer, covered, for 25 minutes. Put into blender and blend until smooth. Return to pan and heat and stir in the cream. Adjust seasoning and serve.

Smoked Chicken and Black Grape Soup

INGREDIENTS:

$1/2$ pt. chicken stock
8 oz. smoked chicken
$1/2$ pt. double cream
4 oz. deseeded black grapes
$1/2$ onion, diced
$1/2$ oz. butter
  Salt and pepper to taste.

METHOD:

Fry onion lightly in butter. Liquidise and add smoked chicken and a little stock. Transfer to pan and add remaining stock and bring to the boil and reduce slightly. Add cream and salt and pepper and grapes. Serve with whipped cream and parsley on top.

BISTRO

Cucumber Salad

INGREDIENTS:

2 cucumbers, peeled and thinly sliced
1 tbsp sugar
3 tbsp vinegar
6 tbsp olive oil
  Salt and pepper
$^1/_2$ pt cream

METHOD:

Sprinkle the cucumber with salt and leave for 1 hour. Liquidise all the other ingredients. Drain the cucumber and mix with the dressing.

Baked Potatoes with Nutmeg

INGREDIENTS:

5 lb. potatoes, peeled
$^1/_2$ pt. cream
$^1/_2$ pt. milk
3 tsp. nutmeg
  Salt and pepper
2 oz. butter.

METHOD:

Cook potatoes in boiling water until soft but not crumbly. Drain and cool. Combine milk and cream with nutmeg and seasoning. Slice potatoes and layer into a greased oven-proof dish putting knobs of butter between layers. Pour the milk and cream mixture over the whole dish and bake in the oven for 30 minutes until golden brown.

Salmon en Papillote

BISTRO

INGREDIENTS:

4 salmon steaks
3 oz. butter
1 glass white wine
3 sprigs chopped dill
3 sprigs chopped tarragon
1 tomato, chopped
1 carrot, cleaned and cut into julienne strips.
1 leek ,cut into julienne strips
$^1/_2$ onion finely chopped.
  Salt and pepper.

METHOD:

Spread out 4 sheeets of greaseproof paper and place knob of butter on each. Place salmon steaks on top of each then scatter equal amounts of vegetables and herbs on top of each steak then top with another knob of butter. Bring up the sides of the greaseproof paper and divide the wine equally onto the salmon. Season and seal up the parcel and bake for approximately 15 minutes at 425F 220C Gas 7.

Leeks with Almonds

INGREDIENTS:

1 lb. leeks
4 oz. butter
4 oz. toasted almonds
  Black pepper

METHOD:

Trim off tops of leeks and roots. Discard the tough outer layer then split them in half lengthways and slice into 1 in. pieces. Melt butter in large pan, add leeks and sauté gently until tender. Toss in toasted almonds and season with black pepper. Place in warm serving dish.

BISTRO

Spanikapita

INGREDIENTS:

1 packet filo pastry
8oz chopped spinach
8oz. cottage cheese
8oz feta cheese
2 cloves garlic, chopped.
1 tsp. oregano
1 tsp. basil
  Seasoning
3 eggs
1 lb. plain flour
1 onion, chopped and fried in 1 oz. of
butter
3 oz. melted butter

METHOD:

Mix all the ingredients together.. Grease a loaf tin with melted butter. Line with 1 layer of filo pastry. Spread on melted butter and repeat until there are 6 layers of filo pastry. Spread over this $^1/_3$ of the filling. Repeat procedure of 6 layers of filo pastry. Add another $^1/_3$ of the filling. Continue until finished. Bake in oven 350f 180C Gas4 for 50 minutes.

Beef and Guinness Casserole

BISTRO

INGREDIENTS:

1 lb. lean beef
4 oz. streaky bacon, diced and crisply
 fried
1 large onion chopped
1 clove garlic crushed
1/2 pt. Guinness stout
2 tsp. oil
1 tsp grated nutmeg)
1 tsp thyme   )   *Tie all herbs*
1 tsp.parsley....... ...)   *together in a*
1 bay leaf............   .)   *piece of muslin*
  Salt and pepper to season
1 tbsp. arrowroot
1 cup, beef stock
1/2 oz butter
1/2 lb. sliced mushrooms
4 pastry boxes (cooked) to finish.

METHOD:

Cut meat into a portion per person (1/2 to 1 ins. thick) Heat oil in heavy pan. Season meat and sear for 2 minutes on both sides in hot oil. Remove from pan. Wipe out pan. Heat butter and sauté onions and mushrooms gently for 3-4 minutes. Put back the meat with fried bacon, stout, garlic and the bag of herbs and stock. Season to taste and cook for 1 1/2 to 2 hours until meat is tender. Remove herbs and thicken with arrowroot.

Warm pastry boxes in oven and serve the beef and sauce on top sprinkled with parsley.

BISTRO

Walnut Tart

INGREDIENTS:

7 oz. plain flour
3 $^1/_2$ oz. ground almonds
2 $^1/_2$ oz. softened butter
3 $^1/_2$ oz. caster sugar
1 egg
1 egg yolk
1 tbsp lemon juice.

METHOD:

Mix all the dry ingredients together and then beat in the eggs, butter and lemon juice. Knead until well mixed and then chill in 'fridge for at least one hour.

FILLING
6 oz. walnuts, chopped
2 eggs
1 $^1/_2$ oz. flour
$^1/_2$ pt. cream.

METHOD:
Blend all ingredients together. Line greased flan tin with pastry and pour filling into flan and bake for 25 minutes until golden brown and firm.

Coffee and Whiskey Cake

CAKE
4 oz. margarine
2 eggs
4 oz. caster sugar
4 oz. self raising flour
$^1/_2$ tbsp. coffee essence

METHOD FOR CAKE:
Combine all ingredients and bake at 350f 180c Gas4 for 35-40 minutes. Leave in tin until cool.

SYRUP
$^3/_4$ pt. water
$^1/_2$ gill strong coffee
4 oz. sugar
$^1/_2$ tbsp. whiskey.

METHOD FOR SYRUP:
Put all ingredients except whiskey into pan and heat until syrupy. Add whiskey. Soak the cake continuously with the syrup before serving.

CHOCOLATE SAUCE
Melt 4 oz. plain chocolate in pan with 1 tablespoon of water.
When serving the cake pour over each slice 2 tablespoons of chocolate sauce and decorate with cream.

Blue Haven

Moules Surprise
Vegetable Terrine with Tomato Coulis

Dublin Bay Gazpacho
Seafood Consommé

Vegetable Chow Mein
Fresh Beetroot au Gratin

Monkfish with Grapefruit
Jean Michel Poulots Baron of Rabbit

Gratinéed Fruits Grand Marnier
Soufflé Glace with Cointreau and Vanilla Sauce

Moules Surprise

BLUE HAVEN

INGREDIENTS:

2 pts. mussels
2 shallots (finely chopped)
1 glass of dry white wine
2 oz. butter
$^1/_2$ pt. of pouring cream
8 puff pastry vol-au-vent cases (small)
1 glass mussel stock
1 tsp. of chopped chives
1 pinch of saffron
1 carrot
6 oz. sea spinach leaves

METHOD:

Cook off the mussels in a little water having first ensured that they are free of grit and sand by scrubbing vigorously under running water with a hard bristle brush. A way of ensuring an even cooking of the mussels is to cover them over with a tea towel before cooking. This steam cooking method is also a little bit faster. Reserve one glass of the mussel stock and discard the rest. Run the cooked mussels under cold water to prevent them cooking further in their own heat and then remove mussels from shells and set aside.

Take a pan and melt the butter. Cook off the chopped shallots gently and add the glass of white wine. Bring to the boil and continue cooking until you have just a spoonful of mixture left in the pan. Add the cream, mussel stock, saffron and bring to the boil. Reduce slightly by cooking for a further $^1/_2$ minute. Add the two pints of mussels and chopped chives and cook for 2 –3 minutes. Season to taste with salt and pepper. Now chop the carrot and sea spinach leaves into a julienne and cook them al dente and set aside.

Place the vol-au-vent pastry cases on a baking tray and line the bases with the carrot/spinach mixture. Fill the cases with mussels and reheat in the oven for a couple of minutes. Remove from oven and place two pastry cases on each plate. Add a little sauce to the cases, place the caps on top and then pour some of the sauce on the plate around the pastry cases.

To garnish, add some pink peppercorns to the sauce and a little sprig of fresh dill or some other herb.

(Sea Spinach grows wild on the road side in proximity to sandy beaches in County Cork.)

Vegetable Terrine with Tomato Coulis

BLUE HAVEN

INGREDIENTS:

1 carrot
1 white turnip
$^1/_4$ swede turnip
4 oz. french beans
2 avocadoes
$^1/_2$ pt. cream.
3-4 leaves gelatine
2 dessertspoons chopped parsley
  Pinch of salt
  Pinch of pepper
  Pinch of nutmeg
  Pinch of caster sugar

Tomato Coulis ingredients:

1 quarter peeled cucumber
1 shallot
3 ripe tomatoes
1 small tin of peeled tomatoes
  Pinch of salt and pepper
  Dash of tabasco

METHOD:

Chop the vegetables finely and cook them off individually in a little water until al dente*.

Peel the two avocadoes and remove flesh from stones. Liquidise with the cream and set aside. Cook off gelatine leaves in a little water with a spoon of cream and add to avocado mixture. Whisk in chopped parsley and season to taste with salt, pepper, nutmeg and caster sugar.

Take a terrine dish and line the bottom with the avocado mixture to a thickness of 1 cm. Next, layer the cooked vegetables individually on top of the avocado base taking care to leave approximately 1 cm. margin around the outer margin of the rectangle. Layer the vegetables in such a way that you have a good colour combination e.g. first carrot then white turnip, another layer of avocado mix, then french beans, then swede turnip and lastly another layer of avocado mix to top it off. Now pour the remainder of the avocado mixture down around the four sides of the terrine(remember that 1 cm. you allowed for earlier). The terrine is now finished and should be placed in the fridge or cold room for twelve hours or so.

METHOD:

Place all ingredients in a liquidiser and blend until smooth. Then refrigerate for a short while.

When ready to serve, slice the terrine, giving two slices per portion. and pour a little of the tomato coulis on the side of the plate. For added effect, add a little creamed horseradish on the other side of the plate and garnish with a sprig of fresh herb.

*See P. 7 for explanation of cookery terms

BLUE HAVEN

Dublin Bay Gazpacho

INGREDIENTS:

8 fresh tomatoes
1lb tin peeled tomatoes
Half cucumber
Medium sized onion
2 celery stalks
2 peppers
Half cup of red wine
Juice of one lemon
16 Large Dublin Bay prawns
8oz ice
Freshly ground black pepper & salt

METHOD:

Put all of the ingredients – except prawns – into a liquidiser and blend. In the meantime, cook off prawns for two minutes in boiling salted water. Cool under running water and remove shell from twelve of the prawn tails. Leave four whole prawns for garnish but remove the shell from the tail section. Pass the soup through a sieve and leave to stand in a fridge for an hour or so. Pour into bowls and garnish with the whole prawns by hanging the prawn over the edge of the soupbowl. Serve the shelled prawn tails on the side and serve with buttered brown soda bread.

Seafood Consommé

INGREDIENTS:

2lbs fish bones
2 –3 onions
2 – 3 carrots
2 bay leaves
8oz fresh salmon
4oz shrimps
2 glasses dry white wine
Salt, Pepper to taste.

METHOD:

Make a fish stock by chopping onions and carrots in a rough dice; add with bay leaves and fish bones into a large pot of cold water and bring to just under the boil. Allow to simmer for 20 to 30 minutes. In the meantime cook the salmon and shrimps in boiling water and then shell the shrimps and cut the salmon into small pieces. Strain off three quarters of the fish stock into a second pot and return to the heat – adding wine, diced fish and season to taste.

Vegetable Chow Mein

BLUE HAVEN

INGREDIENTS:
4 medium carrots
1 large onion
1 green pepper
1 red pepper
8oz. string beans
4 sticks celery
8oz button mushrooms
8oz egg noodles
2 oz. grated roasted peanuts
^{1}/2 cup sesame oil
Soya sauce and oyster sauce to taste.
Some sprigs of fresh herbs.

METHOD:
Dice the vegetables into thin julienne strips and slice the mushrooms. Cook egg noodles in salted water (as per instructions on packet). Now add some sesame oil to a large wok and heat over flame. Add the mixed vegetables and stir fry al dente*, adding soya sauce and oyster sauce to taste. Turn out onto serving dish and sprinkle with grated peanuts. Garnish with fresh herbs and serve with a salad bowl accompaniment.

Fresh Beetroot au Gratin

INGREDIENTS:
8 small beetroot
6 oz. cheddar cheese (red)
2 oz. margarine
1 tbsp. wholemeal flour
^{1}/2 pt. vegetable stock
2 glasses red wine

METHOD:
Boil the beetroot in their skins until tender. Peel them and cut into thick slices and layer in a baking dish. In a separate saucepan make a roux by combining the butter and flour and then add the stock and red wine and cook for two or three minutes, having first brought to the boil. While doing this, grate the cheese and then add half of the cheese to the wine and flour mixture and pour over beetroot. Sprinkle the remainder of the cheese on top and bake in the oven for 20 - 25 minutes at 400F, Gas 6, 200C.

*For explanation of cookery terms see P. 7

Monkfish with Grapefruit

BLUE HAVEN

INGREDIENTS:

28 oz. Monkfish
4 grapefruit
1 shallot
$1/2$ cup of very dry white wine
2 cups fish stock
  Pinch of salt
  Pinch of pepper
$1/2$ pt. of cream.

For Garnish:
some pink peppercorns and one uncooked
tomato, peeled and cut into small cubes.

METHOD:

Peel grapefruit and cut skin into a julienne and set aside. Squeeze grapefruit juice into a saucepan and reduce over a high heat with white wine, fish stock and chopped shallot. Reduce right down until you are left with about 2 dessertspoons of syrup in the saucepan. Now add the cream and bring to the boil. Add the butter and stir well over the heat until sauce is of a smooth constituency.

Cut the Monkfish into approximately five medallions (or slices) per portion. Pan-fry the Monkfish slowly in butter ensuring that you do not over-cook. The fish should retain its own liquid and medallions should be soft when cooked. Arrange the medallions in a circular shape on the plate and garnish by putting a bunch of cooked grapefruit julienne in the centre. Pour the sauce around the fish (not over) and garnish with some pink peppercorns and little cubes of uncooked tomato.

Jean Michel Poulot's Baron of Rabbit

INGREDIENTS:

2 *whole rabbits*
 Rabbit's kidney
 Rabbit's liver
1 *chopped shallot*
1 *cup rabbit stock*
 Pinch of salt
 Pinch of pepper
 A little chopped parsley
$^1/_2$ *breast uncooked chicken*
 A pinch of coriander powder

SAUCE:
1 *cup strong rabbit stock*
1 *half cup of dry white wine*
2 *oz. butter*
 Pinch of salt
 Pinch of pepper

METHOD:

Discard the fore legs. Take the four hind legs and bone out. Now place the bones in a pot of water together with an onion, a carrot and a bay leaf. Bring to the boil and reduce down to make a very strong stock. Reserve the stock for later use. Remove the meat from the carcass so that you are left with the breasts of fillets adhering to the inner skin in one large section. Now prepare the stuffing mixture by chopping the chicken breasts and adding to it the chopped parsley, coriander powder , finely chopped shallot and a pinch of salt and pepper to taste. Add the whole kidneys and liver to the centre of the stuffing mixture and then wrap the breasts around the mixture so that you end up with a "Swiss Roll" shape. Stitch with twine to keep the mixture in place. Set the oven to gas mark 7\8, 220\230C, 425\450F and cook for 8\10 minutes. Oil the four legs, place on a baking tray and cook at the same time together with the kidney and liver.

While the rabbit is cooking in the oven you can now make the sauce. Bring the cup full of strong stock to the boil and to it add a half cup of white wine, 2 oz. butter and salt and pepper to taste. Reduce slightly. When the rabbit is cooked, remove from the oven, slice the separate meat joints and arrange on a plate. Pour sauce on the plate around the meat (not over)and garnish with asparagus spears and spring onions (which have been cooked off al dente in water).

Gratinéed Fruits Grand Marnier

BLUE HAVEN

Assorted fruits peeled and sliced with all pips and skin removed. Any fruit you fancy will do but a combination such as peach, kiwi fruit, strawberry, orange and grapes would do nicely. Refrigerate the fruit after preparation, having set them out on individual sweet plates (either flat plates or something like the old fashioned soup plate would be suitable).

Sabayon Recipe:

INGREDIENTS:
1/2 cup of cream
3 egg yolks
2 dessertspoons sweet white wine.
1 dessertspoon caster sugar
1 dessertspoon lemon juice concentrate
1 liqueur measure Grand Marnier (or Cointreau)

METHOD:
Place all Sabayon ingredients in a stainless steel bowl and whisk briskly in a bain-marie for 10-15 minutes. The warm Sabayon mixture is then poured over the cold fruit and placed under a hot grill for a few seconds, just enough to let the surface of the sauce brown slightly. You will find the combination of the warm Sabayon and the cold fruit absolutely delicious

Soufflé Glace with Cointreau and Vanilla Sauce

INGREDIENTS:
4 egg yolks
6 oz. caster sugar
1/2 glass of water
2 glasses Cointreau
Rind of 2 oranges
3 egg whites
3 oz. caster sugar
1 pt. cream.

For Garnish:
Some powdered cocoa or chocolate, 3\4 brandy snap biscuits per portion.

METHOD:
Cook rind of two oranges with 8 oz. caster sugar and one cup of water for 25/30 minutes slowly. Remove rind and cut into little cubes and set aside.

Cook off 3 oz. caster sugar with 1/2 dessertspoons of water for 20/25 minutes and reduce down until you have a very thick syrup (not quite caramel.)

Make a meringue mixture by beating 3 egg whites for 4/5 minutes until stiff but not hard. Then slowly add the hot thick syrup and whisk briskly into meringue mixture for another few minutes.

Whisk a pint of cream until quite thick.

Cook off 6 oz. caster sugar with a cup of water and make another thick syrup (30 minutes cooking time).

Beat 4 egg yolks and add very hot syrup. Continue beating with whisk for 10 minutes until mixture is cold.

Cottage Loft

Prawn bisque
Nettle soup
Smoked haddock mousse

Brill St Clement
Salmon Danielle

Beansprout salad with sesame oil
Courgette and herb bake

Rock parsnip

Chicken and broccoli casserole
Pigeon breast in red wine
Peking beef

Malibu meringue
Chocolate and raspberry roulade

45

COTTAGE LOFT

Pigeon Breast in Red Wine

INGREDIENTS:

4 Pigeons.
MARINADE:
1 onion chopped/ 1 carrot diced/ 1 stick of celery, chopped
2 cloves of garlic
6 juniper berries
1 tsp sea salt.
6 black peppercorns crushed.
6 fl. oz. red wine.
SAUCE:
Pigeon stock
1 tbsp fruit jelly
1 square dark chocolate.

METHOD:

To make the marinade, fry the carrots, onions, celery, juniper berries and garlic in a little oil for 3 minutes. Add the seasoning and the wine. Bring to the boil and reduce a little. Remove from the heat.
Remove the breasts from the pigeons and make stock from the carcasses. Place the breasts in the marinade and leave overnight.
Heat a non-stick frying pan and cook the breasts for 3-4 minutes on one side. Turn and cook for a further 2-3 minutes until pink (never overcook). Remove pigeon from pan and slice. Add the strained marinade, chocolate and fruit jelly plus 6 tablespoons of pigeon stock to the pan and boil fiercely to reduce to a syrup. Spoon some of the sauce onto a plate and place the sliced pigeon on top.

Smoked Haddock Mousse

INGREDIENTS:

1 lb. smoked haddock
2 hard boiled eggs
1/4 pt. milk
3 tablespoons water
1 onion
1 oz. gelatine
1 oz. roux
* Black pepper 1 bay leaf*
1/4 pt. cream 1/4 pt. mayonnaise

METHOD:

Cook the haddock with the onion in the milk and bay leaf for 10 minutes. Remove the fish and onions from the milk. Discard the bay leaf. Thicken the milk with the roux. Melt the gelatine in the water over low heat. Add the cooked fish, chopped eggs, and gelatine to the cream and mayonnaise and whisk in a bowl. Fold in the thickened milk. Put the mixture into a buttered bowl. Leave to set for 2 - 3 hours. Serve with a little salad and some homemade brown bread.

Prawn Bisque

COTTAGE LOFT

INGREDIENTS:

600 g. prawn shells
2 tbsp. olive oil
2 tbsp Cognac
250 g. carrots)
75 g celery   ) All to be diced
75 g leeks   )
100 g shallots)
3 fresh tomatoes chopped
2-3 cloves of garlic crushed
1 bay leaf
6 juniper berries crushed
   Sprig of tarragon and thyme
2 litres of fish stock or water.
50 g tomato puree
8 fl. oz. double cream
   Salt and black pepper
2 tbsp. butter

METHOD:

Fry the prawn shells in hot oil and flame with
Cognac. Sauté all the other ingredients (except tomato purée and
cream) in butter until soft. Add to the shells with the tomato purée and
pour in the stock. Bring to the boil and simmer, removing the scum
frequently. After 1 hour add the cream and leave to stand for 15
minutes. Strain and serve.

Nettle Soup

INGREDIENTS:

2 Onions peeled and chopped
1 leek washed and chopped
2 large potatoes peeled and sliced
2 oz. butter
4 large cups nettle tops, washed
   Salt and black pepper
   Pinch grated nutmeg.
1 bay leaf
1 ^{1}/2 pt. chicken stock
^{1}/2 pt. milk.

METHOD:

Sauté leeks, onions and potatoes in butter until soft. Add nettles,
pepper, salt, nutmeg and bay leaf. Cook for a further 3-4 minutes. Add
stock and milk. Bring to the boil. Reduce to a slow simmer for about 30
minutes. Remove the bay leaf then sieve or liquidise. Check the
seasoning. Serve topped with a teaspoon of cream.

COTTAGE LOFT

Beansprout Salad with Sesame Oil

INGREDIENTS:

$^1/_2$ medium head of Iceberg lettuce
$^1/_2$ medium cucumber
4 oz. fresh beansprouts
3 small spring onions
  Salt and freshly ground black pepper

DRESSING:
Sesame Oil
Sprinkle of wine vinegar

GARNISH:
Freshly chopped chives

METHOD:

Wash and chop the lettuce and place in a salad bowl. Slice the cucumber and spring onions and add to the salad along with the beansprouts. Season to taste. Toss the salad in the sesame oil and vinegar. Sprinkle with the chopped chives and serve immediately.

Courgette and Herb Bake

INGREDIENTS:

1 $^1/_2$ lb. courgettes
3 tbsp. flour
$^1/_4$ pt. oil
2 onions chopped
1 can of tomatoes (8 oz.)
3 tbsp. tomato purée
1 tsp. dried basil
$^1/_2$ tsp. dried oregano
1 tsp. sugar
  Salt, black pepper
8 oz. Blarney Cheese sliced
$^1/_4$ pt. double cream.

METHOD:

Slice the courgettes into $^1/_2$ ins. slices and toss in the flour. Heat the oil in a frying pan and fry the slices for about 3-4 minutes either side. Remove from pan and drain. Add the onions, tomatoes, the tomato purée, basil, oregano, sugar, salt and pepper to the oil remaining in the pan and cook for 10 minutes. Fold in the whipped cream. Add the courgettes to the tomato mixture and place in a greased casserole dish. Cover with the cheese slices and cook in a moderately hot oven 200C 400F Gas 6 for 20 minutes.

Salmon Danielle

COTTAGE LOFT

INGREDIENTS:

4 slices fresh salmon 3-4 oz. each
8 oz. crabmeat
1 onion
1/2 red pepper chopped
1/2 green pepper chopped
1/2 tsp. curry powder
1 egg
1/4 pt. cream
1 lb. puff pastry
  Salt and pepper

METHOD:

To make stuffing:
Sauté the onions and peppers until soft. Remove from heat. Add the crabmeat, curry powder and seasoning. Mix the cream and egg together and add to the stuffing.

Roll out the pastry. Divide the stuffing and sandwich between two slices of salmon. Wrap in pastry. Glaze the pastry and bake on a lightly greased baking tray in a moderate oven for 25-30 minutes or until golden brown.
Serve the salmon with Béarnaise sauce - See P. 7

Brill St Clement

INGREDIENTS:

2 lb. Brill fillets.
8 oz. peeled prawns
4 slices smoked salmon
4oz. sliced mushrooms
1 onion chopped
3 tbsp. prawn bisque
1 tbsp. Brandy
1 clove garlic crushed
1 tbsp. tarragon
1 tbsp. dill
  Salt and pepper

METHOD:

Cook the onions and garlic in a little oil until golden brown, then add the mushrooms and fry quickly for 2-3 minutes. Spoon the Brandy in and flambé. Add the bisque and herbs then remove from heat. Season to taste. Mix the prawns into this mixture. Butter a loaf tin. Place the Brill fillets in a row with the ends of the fillets turning up over the sides of the tin. Spoon the prawn mixture on top and cover with the slices of smoked salmon. Fold over the Brill fillets from the sides of the tin. Cover with tin foil. Bake in a moderate oven 350F 180C Gas 4 for about 20 minutes.

COTTAGE LOFT

Chicken & Broccoli Casserole

INGREDIENTS:

1 chicken (cooked)
1 lb. broccoli (cooked)
1 large can of condensed mushroom soup
2 tsp. curry powder
2 tbsp. salad cream
4oz crushed rice crispies
  Black pepper
  Pinch cayenne pepper

METHOD:

Strip all the meat off the chicken removing the skin and all bones. Heat the soup, curry powder and salad cream in a pot. Season to taste with the black and cayenne pepper.
Arrange the broccoli on the bottom of a casserole dish. Place the chicken over the broccoli and then pour over the soup mixture. Sprinkle the crushed rice crispies on top when ready to heat. Bake in a moderate to hot oven for 25 minutes or until hot. Serve with a baked potato and salad.

Rock Parsnip

INGREDIENTS:

1 ½ lb. parsnips (thinly sliced)
1 lb. tomatoes (sliced)
3 tbsp. oil
1 oz. butter
1 ½ oz. butter
1 ½ tbsp. brown sugar
  Salt and pepper
4 oz. grated cheddar cheese
½ pt. cream
4 tbsp. breadcrumbs

METHOD:

Heat the oil and fry the parsnip for 3-4 minutes. Grease a casserole dish with half the butter and place a layer of parsnip over the base. Sprinkle with a little sugar, salt and pepper and add a little cream, then cover with a layer of tomatoes. Spread a little more cream and cheese over the tomatoes. Repeat these layers until all the ingredients are used up , finishing with cream and cheese. Top with the breadcrumbs. Cook in the centre of the oven at 325F 170C Gas 3 for about 40 minutes.

Peking Beef

COTTAGE LOFT

INGREDIENTS:

Marinade:
8 cloves garlic crushed
2 tbsp. sugar
$^1/_4$ pt. of water
$^1/_2$ bottle good soya sauce
1 tbsp. oyster sauce
$^1/_2$ tbsp. hot chilli sauce

12 oz. fillet of beef (cut into bite sized strips)
1 onion
1 cooking apple
$^1/_2$ red pepper chopped
$^1/_2$ green pepper chopped
8 oz. cooked rice
8 oz. beansprouts
4 tbsp. sesame oil

METHOD:

First make the marinade. Cook the garlic, sugar and water over a medium heat until a syrup forms. Strain the syrup into a glass bowl adding the soya, oyster and chilli sauces. Place the beef in the marinade for a minimum of 15 minutes - an hour is best.

Heat a heavy-base frying pan until hot then add the sesame oil. Fry the onions, apple and peppers quickly. Add the beef and continue frying. Finally add the rice and beansprouts. Cook for a further minute. Serve at once.

COTTAGE LOFT

Malibu Meringue

INGREDIENTS
4 Meringue nests
 Coconut ice cream
 Malibu Sauce

COCONUT ICE CREAM:
1 pint milk
4 egg yolks 5 oz. coconut freshly grated
1 tbsp. green colouring

MALIBU SAUCE:
$^1/_4$ pt. white wine
1 oz. caster sugar
2 slices of pineapple (peeled and chopped)
1 peach (peeled and chopped)
1 apple (peeled and chopped)
1 plum (peeled and chopped)
1 tbsp. Malibu.

METHOD:
Boil the milk, then leave to cool. Whisk the egg yolks and sugar together. Pour onto the slightly cooled milk. Add the coconut and whisk together. Return to a moderate heat stirring. Allow to cool and infuse for 5 minutes. Add the colouring. Strain through a fine sieve then freeze.

METHOD:
Put all the ingredients except the Malibu into a pan and bring to the boil then cool slightly and liquidise. Add the Malibu.
To Serve: Place a spoonful of ice cream in each meringue. Pour some sauce around the meringue and then arrange a selection of fruits on the sauce.

Chocolate and Raspberry Roulade

INGREDIENTS:
4 oz. Bourneville chocolate
4 eggs
4 oz. caster sugar
2 tsp. instant coffee
1 tbsp. hot water

FILLING:
8 oz. can raspberries
$^1/_2$ pt. cream
1 tbsp. caster sugar
 Chocolate vermicelli

METHOD:
Melt chocolate in a heatproof bowl over a pan of hot water. Dissolve coffee in hot water and mix into melted chocolate. Leave to cool slightly. Separate eggs and whisk yolks with caster sugar. When light and creamy add chocolate and coffee mixture and fold lightly through. Whisk egg whites. When light and fluffy add to chocolate mixture gently folding together. Pour into lightly greased and lined swiss roll tin and bake in the centre of a warm oven 180C 350F Gas 4 for 20 minutes. When cooked, take out of oven and immediately cover with a damp tea towel and leave overnight.
FILLING: Drain raspberries. Whip the cream with caster sugar. Fold raspberries into the stiffly whipped cream. Carefully take roulade from the tin and remove greaseproof paper. Spread filling over the cake and roll up like a swiss roll. Decorate with cream and chocolate vermicelli.

Il Ristorante

Carpaccio

Zuppa Pavese
Pasta e fagioli

Spaghettini ai frutti di mare
Coda di rospo al rosmarino e aglio

Saltimbocca alla Romana

Il Tiramisu
Il gelato alla Crema di Menta

Carpaccio

IL RISTORANTE

INGREDIENTS:

8oz prime fillet beef,very well trimmed
2 leaves iceberg lettuce
2 leaves any other green lettuce

Dressing 1

3 tablespoons home-made mayonnaise
Drop tomato ketchup
Worcester sauce and Cognac to taste
Salt & pepper to season

Dressing 11:

$^1/2$ lemon,squeezed
3 tablespoon high quality olive oil.
Salt & black pepper to season
Very thin slices of Parmiggiano Reggiano
-enough to cover beef
Fresh boletus or any kind of fresh
mushroom,very thinly sliced.

METHOD:

Cut iceberg and lettuce in juliennes and make into a bed on a plate.Cut very thin slices of the beef fillet and place on top . To make the slices very thin place between two sheets of cling-film and beat with the flat side of a wooden hammer.

METHOD:

Mix the ingredients and spread evenly over the slices of raw beef. Sprinkle with chopped chives or parsley.

METHOD:

Mix olive oil,lemon juice and seasoning and place on top of beef 1/2 hour before serving to allow the flavours to mix. Place the slices of Parmesan on top of the meat,next the mushrooms and sprinkle with chopped chives

Wine Suggestion: Chardonnay del Trentino - Santi

Zuppa Pavese

IL RISTORANTE

INGREDIENTS (for 2 people):

1 pint chicken broth
2 eggs,free-range if possible
4 small slices uncut white loaf bread
4 tablespoons fresh parmesan,grated
Finely chopped parsley

METHOD:

Place chicken broth in a saucepan and bring to the boil. In the meantime break the eggs into individual cups. When the broth is boiling,half remove the saucepan from the heat and incline slightly. Gently pour the eggs one after the other into the broth and replace saucepan onto a very gentle heat.
Allow the eggs to poach for a couple of minutes, or more if you prefer. When the eggs are poached remove from the broth and place in the serving dishes. Strain the broth over the eggs so that the eggs are barely covered. Finish off by placing the parmesan on the bread slices and floating on top of the broth. Sprinkle with parsley and serve immediately.

Pasta e Fagioli (Bean and Pasta Soup)

INGREDIENTS:

1 onion,peeled and finely chopped
1 stick celery,finely chopped
1 carrot,finely chopped
1/2 medium leek,finely chopped
Extra virgin olive oil
Olive oil for cooking
200g tinned plum tomatoes with
juice,finely chopped
2 pints home-made beef broth
salt & pepper to season
1 tin Borlotti beans
1/2 tin Cannelloni beans,drained
Small tubular pasta,cooked al dente

METHOD:

Heat olive oil and colour onions in it. Add chopped pork meat and stir for one minute then add remaining vegetables,stirring everything for a few minutes over a low heat. Add chopped tomatoes and juices. Cook for 10-15 minutes. Add Borlotti and Cannelloni,stir for a minute and finally add the broth and cook for 50 -60 minutes. When cooked remove 1/3 of the beans and pass through a mouli or any other type of sieve into the soup. Just before serving add the cooked pasta and finish off by pouring a little extra virgin olive oil on top and a few twists of milled black pepper. If preferred,Parmesan may be sprinkled on top instead of the olive oil & black pepper.

IL RISTORANTE

Spaghettini ai Frutti di Mare

INGREDIENTS (Two persons):

160grs spaghettini
8 mussels
4 cockles
4 clams or 2 tablespoons tinned clams in brine
2 prawns
4 shrimps, out of their shells
1 glass white wine
1 glass fish stock
2 tablespoons tomato sauce
2 cloves garlic, chopped
Parsley
Olive Oil:*

* Only high quality olive oil should be used for cooking.

METHOD:

Brush & clean the molluscs very well and allow to stand under cold running water to remove any sand that may be present. Dry & set aside. Heat the olive oil with the garlic and put mussels, cockles and fresh clams into pan.

Stir once or twice then add the fish stock and white wine. Cover the pan so that the steam will open the mulluscs, then add the tomato sauce, prawns and shrimps. If using tinned clams, these are added at this stage. Do not season at this point. Stir once or twice while reducing the sauce a little. The spaghettini can be cooked in boiled salted water (using sea-salt) until 'al dente'. Strain the spaghettini and add to the sauce in the pan, tossing quickly and not allowing spaghettini to remain long in the sauce, otherwise they will lose their bite. Sprinkle some parsley on the pasta and serve immediately.

NB Parmesan cheese should never be served with this dish

Wine Suggestion: Lacryma Christi del Vesuvio Bianco Doc

Coda di Rospo
al Rosmarino e Aglio

IL RISTORANTE

INGREDIENTS
(For two persons):

8 medallions of monkfish,weighing approx.10oz
1 spray fresh rosemary
2 cloves garlic,finely chopped
1 teaspoonful shallots,finely chopped
Clarified butter and olive oil for cooking
Salt & white pepper for seasoning.

METHOD:

Place equal amounts of butter and oil in a pan and heat. In the meantime , dry the medallions of monkfish,season and toss in white flour. Any excess flour should be shaken off.

Place the fish in the pan,cook for approx.2 mins on each side. Add the rosemary & shallots,cover with foil and place in the oven for 5 minutes at 350F Gas 4 180C.

Remove pan from the oven,add the garlic and allow to sit for 1 minute in the oven before serving.

Wine Suggestion: Creco di Tufo Doc

IL RISTORANTE

Saltimbocca alla Romana

INGREDIENTS (for two people):

*4 scalopinni- ask the butcher to cut very
thin slices from the topside
4 slices Parma Ham
4 leaves fresh sage
Olive oil
Black pepper
Flour
1 glass white wine
4 cocktail sticks*

METHOD:

On each slice* of veal place one slice of parma ham,one leaf of sage and skewer together with the sticks. Season only with black pepper,no salt is required as the ham is salty enough. Lightly toss each scalopinni in flour,shaking off any excess. Heat the oil in a pan and cook the scalopinni for approx 3 minutes. When cooked remove from pan and keep warm. Drain off excess fat from the pan and deglaze with the glass of wine. When reduced pour over saltimbocca before serving.
Finish off by adding a knob of butter.

*To flatten the meat slices place them between two sheets of cling film and beat with the flat side of a wooden hammer.

Wine Suggestion: Rosso Conero Doc San Lorenzo

Il Tiramisu

IL RISTORANTE

INGREDIENTS:

*400g/14oz fresh mascherpone cheese-as
a substitute use 250g/8oz cream cheese
mixed with 1/2pt/300ml double
cream,lightly whipped
5 teaspoons icing sugar
2 egg yolks
2 egg whites,beaten until stiff
24 sponge biscuits
l large cup espresso coffee or very
strong coffee
2oz dark rum
1oz brandy
Cocoa or grated dark chocolate to finish*

METHOD:

Beat mascherpone with icing sugar and egg yolks. If using substitutes,beat the cream cheese and double cream until stiff and add icing sugar and egg yolks and continue beating. Fold in the egg whites.Soak the biscuits in a mixture of espresso,dark rum and brandy. Cover the bottom of a shallow rectangular dish with 12 sponge biscuits. Place $\frac{1}{2}$ the cream mixture on top.

Place the remaining 12 biscuits on top of the cream mixture and then place the remaining mixture on top of these.

Originally the Tiramisu is covered with cocoa powder,but I prefer to use grated dark chocolate which gives a richer flavour.

This dessert should be refrigerated for 24 hours before serving,and may be kept in the 'fridge for up to four days.

Wine Suggestion: Orvieto Antinori Abbocato

IL RISTORANTE

Il Gelato alla Crema di Menta

INGREDIENTS:

5 egg yolks
80gr/4oz castor sugar
500ml/scant pint milk
300 ml/1/2pint double cream,lightly
whipped
20ml/1 teaspoon green creme de menthe

METHOD:

Beat the eggs and sugar until light and frothy. Bring the milk to the boil and pour into egg mixture. Slowly, beating all the time with a whisk. Place the bowl on top of a saucepan with some boiling water in it and cook the custard until the back of a spoon is lightly coated when dipped into the mixture.

Allow the custard to cool,add the creme de menthe and then fold in the cream.

When the mixture is completely cool place in an ice-cream maker for about 40 minutes.

Transfer to a container and keep in the freezer until serving.

Wine Suggestion: Loredan Gasparini Brut

Jim Edwards

Golden fried mushrooms with vegetable mayonnaise
Mussels in garlic breadcrumbs

Mussel chowder
Cream of cauliflower soup

Lamb kidneys with bacon rolls

Salad Creole
Monkfish in fennel and saffron sauce
Symphony of Kinsale seafood

Dressed suprême of chicken with cranberry & lemon sauce
Noisettes of Spring lamb with savoury stuffing

Charlotte Royale
Meringue surprise

JIM EDWARDS

Golden Fried Mushrooms with Vegetable Mayonnaise

METHOD:
Choose 32 medium sized mushrooms, wipe clean and leave 1/2 the stem on. Dust in flour then dip in egg and coat with soft white breadcrumbs.

TO PREPARE MAYONNAISE:
Use home-made or a good brand of prepared mayonnaise. Deep-fry 2 deseeded red peppers. Skin and put through a sieve or liquidiser. Add to mayonnaise until pink in colour. Add some crushed garlic.

Spread mixture on 4 plates and arrange 8 mushrooms in a circle stems upright. Garnish with sprigs of parsley in the centre of the circle.

Mussels in Garlic Breadcrumbs

INGREDIENTS:

3 pts. mussels

White breadcrumbs

2 cloves of garlic (crushed)
Chopped parsley
4oz. melted butter

METHOD:

Scrub mussels. Clean and remove beard with sharp knife. Steam open in a large covered pan with 1 pint of water and a glass of dry white wine. When mussels start to open, shake saucepan and remove from heat. Discard mussels which have not opened.
While mussels are cooking prepare the stuffing.
Add the parsley to the breadcrumbs and a little salt and pepper to taste. Mix the crushed garlic with the melted butter and pour over the breadcrumb mixture.
Return to mussels and drain off cooking liquid (can be reserved for mussel chowder).
Discard $^1/_2$ shell of each mussel and top the remaining with garlic breadcrumbs. Brown under the grill. Serve with a wedge of lemon and brown soda bread.

Mussel Chowder

JIM EDWARDS

INGREDIENTS:

2 pts. mussels
1 onion, chopped finely
2 cloves garlic, crushed
2 oz. butter
1 bay leaf
$^1/_2$ pt. dry white wine
1 pt. chicken stock
4 celery sticks sliced thinly
2 leeks shredded thinly.

METHOD:

Scrub mussels well and remove beards. Fry onion and garlic in butter using a large saucepan. Add wine and bay leaf and bring to the boil. Add mussels, cover and boil until mussels are open. Strain the mussels through a colander and return the liquid to a clean saucepan. Shell the mussels and set aside. Add stock to the mussel broth. Season with salt and pepper. Add leeks and celery and simmer for 15 minutes. Add the mussels, cover and simmer, do not boil. Serve garnished with parsley and garlic bread on the side.

Cream of Cauliflower Soup

INGREDIENTS:

1 cauliflower
2 large potatoes peeled and diced
$^1/_2$ pt. hot milk
1 pt. chicken stock
$^1/_4$ pt. single cream
 Salt and grated nutmeg
$^1/_2$ oz. butter

METHOD:

Simmer cauliflower and potatoes in boiling stock for 20 minutes. Purée the mixture in a liquidiser and return to saucepan. Add milk and cream. Season with salt and nutmeg. Reheat. Garnish with small croûtons of fried bread.

JIM EDWARDS

Symphony of Kinsale Seafood

INGREDIENTS:

10 oz. Turbot
8 oz. Salmon
8 oz. Monkfish
8 Scallops
16 Mussels
16 fresh Prawns

SAUCE:

2 shallots chopped
1 glass dry Vermouth
¹/₄ pt. fish stock
¹/₄ pt. double cream
2 oz. butter
¹/₂ tsp. fresh dill

METHOD:

Fry shallots in 1oz. of butter. Add fish stock and Vermouth. Cut the fish into chunks of the same size and poach gently until cooked. Remove and keep warm. Reduce the cooking liquid and add the cream. Boil until thickened then whisk in remaining butter. Arrange the fish on 4 hot plates and pour the sauce around the fish. Garnish to your liking.

Monkfish in Fennel and Saffron Sauce

INGREDIENTS:

2 lbs Monkfish sliced
¹/₄ pt. cream
1 oz. shallots finely chopped
  Fresh fennel
1 glass dry white wine
6 strands of saffron infused in a little water
¹/₄ pt. fish stock
1 oz. butter

METHOD:

Poach the Monkfish gently by placing in a large pan with a little water and wine and some seasoning. Cover with foil and put over a slow heat. When cooked remove and keep warm.
To make the sauce, sauté until soft but not brown the shallots and finely chopped fennel. Add fish stock and remaining wine. Reduce by half. Pour in the saffron and add cream. Again slowly reduce. For a nice touch finish with a small amount of butter at the very end. Pour over the Monkfish and garnish with a sprig of fresh fennel.

64

Lamb Kidneys with Bacon Rolls

JIM EDWARDS

INGREDIENTS:

8 lambs' kidneys
1 ¹/₂oz. flour
  Salt and pepper
2 oz. butter
4 oz. mushrooms, sliced
1 clove garlic, crushed
1 lb. tomatoes, peeled and chopped
3 tbsp. of sweet sherry
¹/₂ tbsp. chopped fresh basil
8 slices of smoked streaky bacon
4 slices of toast.

METHOD:

Remove core and any fat from the kidneys and cut into slices. Wash, then drain dry. Coat kidneys with seasoned flour and brown in hot butter. Place in casserole dish. Add mushrooms and garlic to remaining fat and cook for 2-3 minutes then put with the kidneys. Add basil. Add any remaining flour to the pan in which mushrooms were cooked and mix well. Add tomatoes, sherry and a little stock. Bring to boiling point stirring. Pour over the ingredients in the casserole. Cover and cook in a low heat for 40 minutes. Fry the bacon lightly. Roll and finish off under the grill. To serve as a starter place two triangles of toast on each of the four hot plates (points together) and spoon kidneys and sauce on to the toast and arrange the bacon rolls beside each triangle with fresh basil. For luncheon serve with a side salad and spaghetti.

Salad Creole

INGREDIENTS:

20 medium-sized prawns (cooked and
  shelled)
4 small ripe melons
1 pinch of ground ginger
  (curry powder may be used instead)
8 oz. boiled rice well drained
4 tbsp. of double cream
1 tbsp. of lemon juice
  Salt

METHOD:

Slice off the stem ends of the melons and reserve for later use. Scoop out the melon seeds and discard. Carefully scoop out the flesh with a spoon and dice. Season with salt and ginger. Add the rice and mix together. Chill. At the last minute add the cream, prawns and lemon juice. Refill the hollowed melons with the mixture and replace lids

JIM EDWARDS

Dressed Suprême of Chicken
with Cranberry and Lemon Sauce

INGREDIENTS:

4 chicken breasts skinned
6 oz. butter
 Juice and jest of a whole orange
1 clove of garlic crushed
2 oz. breadcrumbs
 Seasoned flour
2 eggs
8 oz. cranberries
 Juice and zest of 1 lemon
3oz. sugar

METHOD:

Stuff the pocket of chicken breasts with light garlic butter to which you have added the orange zest. Coat lightly in seasoned flour, dip in beaten egg and coat with breadcrumbs. Place the chicken breasts in a large pan and sauté gently in butter until cooked throughout.

CRANBERRY AND LEMON SAUCE:

Place the cranberries in a litter water and sugar in a pan and bring to the boil. Reduce heat and add lemon and orange juice and lemon zest and simmer until fruit breaks down and is of a liquid consistency.
Place chicken in the centre of a plate with cranberry sauce on one side and alternate slices of orange and lemon on the other.

Noisettes of Spring Lamb
with Savoury Stuffing

JIM EDWARDS

INGREDIENTS:

2 loins of lamb weighing 1^1/2lb. approximately after boning and trimming

STUFFING:
4 oz. lean veal minced
6 oz. breadcrumbs
  Fresh thyme and parsley
1 whole onion chopped finely
1 clove of garlic crushed
2 oz. butter.

SAUCE:
^{1}/2 pt. demi glace
2 oz. finely diced shallots
^{1}/2 gill Crème de Cassis
  Fresh mint

METHOD:

Stuffing: Fry onion and garlic together in butter until transparent. Add minced veal and herbs and brown lightly. Add breadcrumbs. Season with salt and pepper and mix well.
Batten loin slightly and fill with stuffing mixture. Roll and secure with thread or cocktail sticks. Cook loins in medium oven for 30 minutes approximately. Slice, giving approximately 3 noisettes per person .

Sauce:
Sauté shallots, add chopped mint and Crème de Cassis and reduce. Add demi-glace* and reduce again.
To serve arrange noisettes down centre of the plate and serve with Cassis Sauce.

*For demi-glace see P. 7

67

JIM EDWARDS

Charlotte Royale

INGREDIENTS:

1 pt. milk.
4 eggs separated
4 oz. sugar
$^1/_4$ pt. cream
1 leaf gelatine
  Vanilla Pod
1 swiss roll sliced
$^1/_4$ pt. fruit jelly.

METHOD:

Bring milk and vanilla pod to the boil. Remove pod. Slowly pour the milk onto the egg yolks and sugar stirring all the time. Return to the stove and cook carefully. Do not boil. Continue cooking without boiling until mixture coats the back of a spoon. Add the soaked gelatine and allow to dissolve. Sit on some ice and when just ready to set fold in the whipped cream followed by the stiffly beaten egg white. Prepare charlotte mould by setting 1 cm. of jelly in the bottom and line with sliced swiss roll. Fill the mould with the mix and allow to set in the fridge. When set, gently warm the mould and turn out on a large plate. Decorate as desired.

Meringue Surprise

INGREDIENTS:

3 egg whites
6 oz. caster sugar

FILLING:
8 oz. cream cheese
1/4 pt. double cream
3 tbsp caster sugar
16 oz. strawberries
  A few drops of Kirsch

METHOD:

Meringues: Whisk the egg whites until they stand in peaks. Whisk in half the sugar until the mixture thickens. Fold in the remaining sugar carefully. Fill a piping bag and on a greased baking sheet. Create nests by moving the bag in a whirling movement. Bake in a very cool oven for 3 hours.
Filling: Mash the cream cheese in a bowl and add cream and sugar. Make a purée by passing 8 oz. strawberries through a sieve. Add the purée to the cream cheese mixture and flavour to taste with Kirsch. Fill cavity of meringues with mixture and arrange the remaining strawberries sliced porcupine style on top. Decorate with piped cream and whole strawberries.

Man Friday

Smoked salmon mousse with cucumber
Kinsale hot oysters

Cream of courgette and leek soup
Seafood chowder

Potato and leek pie
Mushrooms cooked in the oven

Turbot Daniel
Sole stuffed with prawn, crab and leeks

Chicken Printanier
Fillet of beef with tarragon and mustard

Lemon tart
Crème de Menthe chocolate cup

MAN FRIDAY

Smoked Salmon Mousse with Cucumber

INGREDIENTS:

10 ozs. smoked salmon
$^1/_3$ pint of homemade mayonnaise
2 tbsp. warm water
$^1/_3$ pint cream
3 egg whites
Juice of 2 lemons
Black pepper
1 cucumber
1 tsp. white wine vinegar

METHOD:

Soak the gelatine in warm water until dissolved. Roughly chop the smoked salmon. Put smoked salmon, mayonnaise, cream, lemon juice and gelatine in a food processor or electric blender. Purée until smooth. Whisk egg whites and fold into smoked salmon mixture. Spoon mixture into six dampened moulds.

Peel and coarsely grate cucumber. Place the cucumber in a colander. Sprinkle with salt and vinegar and leave to sweat for 30 minutes. Press out excess moisture and pat dry with kitchen paper. Turn out moulds. Sprinkle with a little paprika and surround with cucumber.

Kinsale Hot Oysters

INGREDIENTS (For Two Persons):

12 Oysters
$^1/_4$ pint beurre blanc sauce
Julienne strips of vegetables (e.g. carrots, courgettes and celery)
2-3 tbsp. cream.
Freshly ground black pepper

METHOD:

Open oysters over a small saucepan catching all the liquid. Detach the oysters and put them into the saucepan with the liquid. Heat oysters in liquid for about 30 seconds. Remove and keep hot in their half shell. Reduce liquid. Add Cream and beurre blanc* sauce, julienne of vegetables and pepper. Do not boil. Pour a little sauce over each oyster and serve with lemon immediately.

* For beurre blanc, see P. 7

Cream of Courgette and Leek Soup

MAN FRIDAY

INGREDIENTS:

8 Leeks, chopped
8 courgettes, chopped
2 potatoes, chopped
1 onion, chopped
1 $\frac{1}{2}$ pts chicken stock
$\frac{1}{2}$ pt. cream
2 oz. butter
Salt and pepper

METHOD:

Melt butter in a heavy saucepan. Add leeks, onion, potatoes and season with salt and pepper. Sweat for about 5 minutes. Add courgettes, sweat for another 5 minutes. Add stock. Cook for 10-15 minutes until vegetables are soft. Liquidise. Add cream and adjust seasoning.

Seafood Chowder

INGREDIENTS:

1 lb. monkfish
1 lb. prawns - uncooked and peeled
12 large mussels
1 carrot)
1 onion)
1 leek) Cut into strips
1 stick celery)
1 small courgette)
2 cloves of garlic - crushed
4 fl. ozs. dry white wine.
2 sprigs of thyme
1 $\frac{1}{2}$ pts good fish stock
$\frac{1}{2}$ pt. prawn stock
1oz. butter
2 tbsp. chopped parsley
$\frac{1}{4}$ pt. cream.

METHOD:

Melt butter in a heavy saucepan. Add vegetables, garlic and thyme. Sweat for 5 minutes. Add wine and reduce by half. Add stock and simmer for 10 minutes. Add monkfish. Cook for 2-3 minutes. Then add prawns and mussels. Just before serving add cream and chopped parsley.

Potato and Leek Pie

MAN FRIDAY

INGREDIENTS :

1 lb. potatoes
8 leeks
2 oz. butter
2 cloves garlic - crushed
$^1/_2$ lb. grated cheese
$^1/_2$ pt. cream.
Salt and pepper

METHOD:

Wash leeks and cut into thin rounds. Peel and slice potatoes to same thickness as leeks. Sauté leeks and garlic in 1 oz. butter for two minutes . Use the remaining butter to grease a casserole dish. Arrange a layer of sliced potatoes, leeks and cheese. Season. Repeat layers 2 - 3 times. Add cream. Cover and bake in hot oven for $^1/_2$ hour. Five minutes before cooked remove casserole cover and brown top of pie.

Mushrooms Cooked in the Oven

One of the simplest and nicest ways of cooking mushrooms is to lay them on a greased ovenproof dish with a spot of butter and a teaspoon of cream inside each cap.
Season well. Cover closely first with paper then with a lid and cook them in the oven, keeping all the flavour and fragrance of the mushroom. Remove lid only immediately before serving.

Turbot Daniel

MAN FRIDAY

INGREDIENTS:

1 lb. 4 oz. large turbot fillets.
20 large Dublin Bay Prawns
2 shallots
^{1}/2 pt. fish fumet (fish stock).
6 tbsp. dry white wine (e.g. Sancerre)
3 tbsp. Vermouth
^{2}/3 pt. of cream
2 oz. butter
Juice of ^{1}/2 lemon.
2 chopped tomatoes peeled with seeds removed

METHOD:

Remove skin from turbot fillets. Peel prawns.
Put the fish fumet, white wine, vermouth, chopped shallots and pinch of salt in a sauté pan. Bring to the boil and add turbot fillets. Reduce heat, simmer for 3-4 minutes.
Take out fish and keep hot. Bring liquid back to boil, add prawns and cook for 30 seconds. Remove the prawns from the liquid and keep hot. Reduce the cooking liquid to a glistening syrup. Add cream. Reduce until sauce is slightly thickened. Remove from heat and incorporate butter in small pieces. Add chopped tomatoes and lemon juice to taste. To serve spoon sauce over bottom of large heated plates. Arrange turbot fillets and prawns on top.
Serve immediately.

73

MAN FRIDAY

Sole Stuffed
with Prawn, Crab and Leeks

INGREDIENTS:

4 black sole - ³/₄ to 1 lb. each.
¹/₂ lb. cooked fresh white crab meat.
16 large Dublin Bay Prawns.
2 whites of leeks.
¹/₄ pt. of white dry wine
¹/₄ pt. fish stock
2 tbsp. Noilly Prat
¹/₂ pt. cream.
4 oz. butter
Juice and grated rind of ¹/₂ lemon

METHOD:

Skin and fillet sole. Leave aside. Slice leeks finely and sweat in 1 oz. of butter with salt and pepper. Shell prawns. Butter a shallow ovenproof baking dish. Place two fillets of each sole on baking dish. Arrange leeks, crab meat and prawns on top. Lay the remaining fillets of sole around filling to form boat shapes. Add white wine,Noilly Prat, fish stock, juice and grated rind of lemon,salt and pepper. Cover dish. Bake in a hot oven for about 5 minutes. When cooked remove fish and keep warm. Strain fish juice and reduce to a 1/4. Add cream. Reduce again until sauce is slightly thickened. Remove from heat and beat in 3 oz. of butter. Arrange fish on 4 large plates. Spoon sauce over fish and gratinate under a grill. Serve immediately.

Chicken Printanier

MAN FRIDAY

INGREDIENTS:

4 chicken breasts
1 small carrot
$^1/_2$ small onion.
1 stick celery - all finely chopped
$^1/_2$ small courgette - finely chopped
1 sprig tarragon - 1 sprig thyme
16 large prawns cooked and peeled.
1 oz. butter
1 tbsp. chopped chives
1 tbsp. basil
$^1/_2$ pt. chicken flavoured beurre blanc

METHOD:

Season and cook all chopped vegetables in 1 oz. butter with thyme and tarragon for two minutes and cool. Cut a pocket in each chicken breast and season. Mix cooked prawns with vegetables and stuff into chicken breast. Place in buttered seasoned tin foil. Seal well and bake in oven for 15-20 minutes. Combine basil and chives with beurre blanc* sauce. Slice chicken breasts and arrange on plate with sauce.

* For beurre blanc, see P. 7

Fillet of Beef with Tarragon and Mustard

INGREDIENTS:

4 fillet steaks about 8 - 10 oz. each
1 shallot finely chopped
1 clove garlic crushed
2 tbsp. finely chopped tarragon
1 tsp. English mustard
12 fl. oz. beef stock
1 oz. butter
4 fl. oz. white wine
Salt and freshly ground black pepper

METHOD:

Season fillets with salt and pepper. Saute in a hot non-stick pan for about 3-4 minutes on each side. Remove from pan and keep hot. Add shallots and garlic to pan and saute until transparent. Add white wine and reduce. Add stock and reduce by half. Stir in mustard, tarragon, butter and serve.

Lemon Tart

MAN FRIDAY

INGREDIENTS:

1 ¹/₂ lbs. short bread pastry.
Juice and grated rind of four lemons.
8 eggs.
12 oz. sugar.
¹/₂ pt. cream.

METHOD:

Roll out the pastry and line an 8 ¹/₂ in. greased flan ring with the pastry. Bake blind for 10-15 minutes in preheated oven 200C 400F or Gas 6. Whisk eggs. Add sugar. Stir in juice and grated rind of lemons. Add slightly whisked cream. Pour into pastry case. Bake for 45 minutes to 1 hour at 150C 300F or gas 3. Allow to cool before removing ring from tart.

Crème de Menthe Chocolate Cup

INGREDIENTS:

¹/₂ lb. dark good quality chocolate.
3 oz. grated chocolate.
1 pt. home made Crème de Menthe ice cream.
¹/₂ pt. whipped cream.
1 glass Crème de Menthe.

METHOD:

Melt chocolate and line 8 paper baking cases with melted chocolate. Allow to harden. Mix 2 oz. grated chocolate with ice cream. Remove paper from chocolate cups. Fill with ice cream. Pipe some whipped cream on top. Pour the Crème de Menthe over each chocolate cup and decorate with the remaining grated chocolate.

Max's Wine Bar

Spinach pasta with salmon
Pear and blue cheese salad

Nut soup
Curried parsnip soup

Chopped raw vegetables and fruit with yogurt dressing

Fish pie
Monkfish in tarragon and white wine

Liver with pineapple and cheese
Creamed leeks

Orange caramel cream
Chocolate rum mousse

Spinach Pasta with Salmon

MAX'S WINE BAR

INGREDIENTS:

Small piece of cooked fresh salmon
Spinach pasta
Cream
White wine

METHOD:

Drop pasta in large pan of boiling salted water. While it is cooking flake the salmon. Melt butter in a large frying pan. Add cream and white wine and reduce to thicken.. Drain pasta. Toss in frying pan with cream and salmon flakes. Adjust seasoning and serve with freshly grated parmesan cheese.

Pear and Blue Cheese Salad

INGREDIENTS:

1 large dessert pear
1 piece of blue cheese
Salad greens
French dressing
Cress

METHOD:

Wash and dry salad and arrange on individual plates. Chop pear into small dice leaving skin on. Crumble or dice the cheese. Scatter mixture of both on each plate. Garnish with a little cress. Pass the French dressing with the salad.

Nut Soup

MAX'S WINE BAR

INGREDIENTS

3 cups chicken stock
^{1}/2 cup of salted peanuts
^{1}/2 tsp. chilli powder or dash of Tabasco
1 cup milk
  Salt and pepper

METHOD:

Bring stock to the boil. Add peanuts. Cook over moderate heat for about 5 minutes. Add chilli or tabasco. Pour into blender and blend until smooth. Rinse out blender with milk. Add to peanut mixture and bring to the boil. Serve hot with croutons or chilled with cucumber slices floating on top.

Curried Parsnip Soup

INGREDIENTS:

4 large parsnips peeled and sliced
4 large onions roughly chopped
3 cups of strong chicken stock
1 tbsp. hot powder
  Juice of ^{1}/2 lemon
  Milk
  Salt and Pepper
  Plain yogurt or cream

METHOD:

Pressure cook or steam parsnip and onions until soft. Purée in blender with chicken stock and milk until smooth. Return to a saucepan. Add curry powder and lemon juice. Add milk to obtain required consistency. Bring to the boil and simmer for 10 minutes.
Adjust seasoning. Serve with thick swirl of cream or yogurt on top.

MAX'S WINE BAR

Chopped Raw Vegetables and Fruit with Yogurt Dressing

INGREDIENTS:

Assorted raw vegetables e.g. carrots, cauliflower sprigs, runner beans, turnip, radishes etc.
Fresh fruit e.g. apples, pears grapes, kiwi.
Dried fruit and nuts (as bought ready-mixed)
Sunflower seeds
Lettuce Leaves

DRESSING:
5 oz. natural yogurt
2 tsp. honey
1 tsp. lemon juice
 Salt and pepper
 Large pinch Cayenne pepper

METHOD:

Chop raw vegetables and fruit reasonably coarsely. Whisk yogurt dressing in bowl and fold in vegetables and fruit. Line individual plates with lettuce leaves and pile on vegetable/fruit mixture. Coarsely chop dried fruit and nuts with grinder blade of food processor. Sprinkle on top of vegetables and fruit along with sunflower seeds.

Fish Pie

MAX'S WINE BAR

INGREDIENTS:

6 lbs. cod
2 lb. smoked haddock
1 lb. prawns
4 pt. milk
3 bay leaves
8 oz. butter
4 oz. flour
6 tbsp chopped parsley
  Juice of one lemon
4 hard boiled eggs roughly chopped

POTATO TOPPING:
4 lb. boiled potatoes
2 oz. butter
$^1/_2$ pt. soured cream
  Nutmeg
  Salt pepper
  Grated cheddar cheese

METHOD:

Simmer fish in one pint of milk to which has been added bay leaves plus a few flecks of butter. When cooked pour off liquid and reserve. Skin and bone fish and flake into largish pieces.

To make the sauce melt butter, stir in flour, cook for a minute or two and gradually add fish liquor and remaining milk. Season. Mix together fish, prawns and sauce along with the eggs, parsley and lemon juice. Pour mixture into baking dish. Cream the potatoes while hot adding butter and soured cream. Season and add nutmeg to taste. Spread evenly over fish and sprinkle with grated cheese. Bake in oven for 20 minutes or until cheese is golden brown.

MAX'S WINE BAR

Monkfish in Tarragon and White Wine

INGREDIENTS:

1 ¹/₂ lbs. Monkfish
4 tbsp dry white wine
¹/₂ pt. cream
  Butter
  Tarragon
  Salt and pepper

METHOD:

Cut monkfish into bite sized pieces, discarding any gristle. Melt butter in large pan and gently saute monk fish until opaque and almost cooked. Add cream, wine and tarragon and turn up heat to reduce to required consistency i.e. just coating the fish pieces. A touch of concentrated fish stock enhances the flavour. Garnish with fresh tarragon if possible or sprig of other suitable herb e.g. fennel. Served with creamed or new potatoes and vegetables of choice.

Liver with Pineapple and Cheese

MAX'S WINE BAR

INGREDIENTS:

Calves Liver
Pineapple rings (1 per portion)
Cheddar Cheese in slices large enough
to cover pineapple
Butter

METHOD:

Heat butter in frying pan. Pre-heat grill. Quickly fry liver slices to taste. Meanwhile arrange pineapple slices topped with a slice of cheese in grill pan and place under grill until cheese is melting. Using a fish slice place pineapple and cheese on top of liver on individual plates and serve with whatever most appeals as accompaniment. Grilled bacon and creamed potatoes suit very well.

Creamed Leeks

INGREDIENTS:

Leeks
Cream
Butter
Nutmeg

METHOD:
Cut off coarse part of green and discard damaged bruised or outer leaves of leeks. Slice them vertically in half (this ensures that all grit is removed) then chop in inch lengths. Wash thoroughly and drain. Melt butter in pan and toss in leeks and cook rapidly for 1 minute. Add cream and salt and pepper and freshly grated nutmeg. Stir while cream reduces. Serve while leeks are still slightly crisp.

Orange Caramel Cream

MAX'S WINE BAR

INGREDIENTS:

Caramel:
100 gr. sugar
60 ml. water

Orange Cream:
500 ml. heavy cream
Grated rind of two oranges
3 eggs
4 egg yolks
160 gr. sugar
375 ml orange juice
60 ml. cointreau

METHOD:

In a heavy saucepan cook sugar and water over a low heat stirring constantly until dissolved. Raise heat and boil without stirring until mixture is golden brown. Quickly pour into each ramekin to cover bottom. Cool until set.

Scald cream with orange rind. Whisk yolks and eggs in bowl and add sugar. Whisk in orange juice and Cointreau. Gradually pour in hot cream whisking constantly. Pour mixture over caramel to fill ramekins. Place in bain marie, cover with foil and bake for 1 to 1 $\frac{1}{2}$ hours to 150C 330F Gas 2 - water must be hot but not boiling. A folded tea towel under ramekins helps keep temperature down. When cooked cool to room temperature and chill.

To serve unmould custards and decorate with orange slices and mint leaves.

Chocolate Rum Mousse

INGREDIENTS:

12 oz. dark chocolate
3 cap-fulls dark rum
6 eggs

METHOD:

Separate the eggs. Whisk whites until stiff. Melt chocolate in a double boiler or over a pan of boiling water or in a microwave oven. Beat in the egg yolks and the rum until the chocolate mixture is smooth. Fold together stiffly beaten egg whites and chocolate with a light lifting motion. Do not over blend. Chill until firm. Serve with a blob of cream.

Trident Hotel

Oysters with watercress
Mussel terrine

Carrot and orange soup
Chilled strawberry soup

Gratin of turnips
Mange-tout with lemon

Scallops with dill

Noisettes of lamb with tarragon

Orange and strawberry surprise
Cointreau and chocolate mousse

TRIDENT HOTEL

Oysters with Watercress

INGREDIENTS:

24 Oysters
Lemon Juice
6 Shallots very finely chopped
2 tsp. white wine vinegar
10oz butter, diced
Freshly ground white pepper and sea salt.
$^1/_2$ oz butter
4oz spinach sliced.
2oz watercress leaves
24 small spinach leaves.

For the Garnish:
Julienne of cucumber
Chopped chives
Radicchio Leaves
Mint Leaves

METHOD:

Open oysters and strain the juices into a pan. Add a squeeze of lemon juice and bring to just below simmering point. Add the oysters and heat for about 45 seconds. Transfer to a lightly warmed plate with a slotted spoon. Cover. Wash the oyster shells and put in a low oven. Simmer the shallots in the vinegar and half the oyster cooking juices until nearly all the liquid has evaporated. Reduce the heat to very low and gradually whisk in 300 gr.\10 oz. butter making sure each piece is fully incorporated before adding the next. Season with white pepper and a little of the remaining juice as necessary. Meanwhile heat the $^1/_2$oz butter in a small pan. Add the spinach and watercress and cook until soft. Increase the heat to drive off the excess moisture. Purée then season adding a squeeze of lemon juice if necessary. Keep warm over a low heat. Place the small spinach leaves and cucumber julienne in the top half of a steamer or a colander. Bring a pan of salted water to the boil. Cover with the top half of the steamer or the colander. Cover and steam for 30 seconds. Line the oyster shells with the spinach leaves, add the watercress and spinach purée, then the sauce and finally the oysters. Garnish with cucumber julienne and chives.
Arrange radicchio and mint leaves around.

Mussel Terrine

TRIDENT HOTEL

INGREDIENTS:

8oz. mussels in their shells
2 fl. oz. dry white wine.
1 tsp chopped parsley
1 tsp chopped chives
8oz turbot chopped and chilled
 Salt
 Lemon Juice
 1 egg white
8 fl. oz. double cream chilled
 Freshly ground white pepper
1 green pepper blanched and diced
6 spinach leaves trimmed and blanched
2 oz. cooked prawns shelled

Sauce:
Flesh of two ripe tomatoes
^{1}/2 tbsp. tarragon vinegar
^{1}/2 tsp. tomato puree
1 tbsp. olive oil.
 Pinch of sugar
 Salt
 Freshly ground white pepper

Garnish:
Coriander or flat parsley leaves and
tomato rose.

METHOD:

Cook the mussels with wine and herbs in a covered heavy based pan over a high heat for about 5 mins shaking the pan frequently until they open. Discard any that remain closed and remove the others from their shells. Dry on absorbent paper. Blend the turbot in a food processor. Then mix in the salt and lemon juice followed by the egg white. Pass through a sieve into a bowl placed over a bowl of ice. Then gradually work in the cream. Add white pepper, cover and chill for 30 minutes.
Heat oven to 150C 300F Gas 2.
Line the base of a terrine with buttered greaseproof paper. Divide the turbot mixture into ^{2}/3 and ^{1}/3. Fold the green pepper into the larger portion and spread half of this in the base of the terrine. Cover with half the spinach leaves and lay half the mussels over them.
Fold the prawns into the remaining spinach leaves. Spread the remaining green pepper mixture over the spinach leaves. Cover with buttered greaseproof paper and stand the terrine in a roasting or baking tin. Pour in boiling water to surround the terrine and place in the oven for 1 hour.

SAUCE METHOD:
Purée the tomatoes vinegar and oil for the sauce, then add the tomato puree sugar and seasoning to taste and to adjust the colour. Purée again and chill. Allow the terrine to cool slightly before unmoulding. Cut the terrine into slices. Place one on each plate and place a spoonful of the sauce to the side.
Garnish with coriander or flat parsley leaves and tomato rose.

Carrot & Orange Soup

TRIDENT HOTEL

INGREDIENTS:

2 lbs carrots,peeled & sliced
2 lbs potatoes,peeled and sliced
4 medium onions,sliced
3 oranges
4 oz butter
6 oz flour
12 pints cold water

Method:

Remove the rind and juice from the oranges
Melt the butter in a saucepan and sauté the rind of oranges,carrot and onion until onion is soft but not brown. Add the flour and stir for one minute. Add the juice of the oranges and water. Bring to the boil and add in the sliced potatoes. Simmer for 30-40 minutes. Blend the soup and season to taste.
When serving sprinkle with a little cream and zest of orange.

Chilled Strawberry Soup

INGREDIENTS:
10lbs strawberries,washed
1 bottle white wine
4 bottles soda water
3-4 glasses liqueur of your choice

Method:
Blend half the amount of strawberries and dice the other half.
Mix all the ingredients together and chill for one hour. Serve in well chilled bowls and sprinkle with diced plain biscuit.

Mange-tout with lemon.

TRIDENT HOTEL

INGREDIENTS:

1 lb small Mange-tout ,topped and tailed,
washed and drained
3 ¹/₂ pints water
2oz unsalted butter
Juice of half a lemon
Salt & freshly ground white pepper

METHOD:

Boil the water with 2 tablespoons salt
Place the mange-tout in the water and boil for 2 minutes. Refresh by running plenty of cold water over them and drain. Heat the butter in a saucepan and season with salt & pepper. Add the mange-tout,cover and cook for a few seconds. Remove the lid and cook for a further minute until the mange-tout are coated with a film of butter. Stir in the lemon juice, correct the seasoning and serve immediately as the lemon juice can discolour this vegetable.

Gratin of Turnips

INGREDIENTS:

2lb Turnips,peeled & thinly sliced
12 fl.oz whipped cream
1 bay leaf
1 sprig thyme
3-4 white peppercorns,crushed
1 clove garlic
Dash of white wine vinegar

METHOD:

Pre-heat oven to 180C/350F/Gas 5. Boil the cream with the bay leaf, thyme ,peppercorns, garlic, vinegar and pinch of salt for 2-3 minutes. Place the turnips overlapping in an ovenproof dish. Strain the cream over them and press down. Place in the oven and bake for 20 minutes. Serve hot.

TRIDENT HOTEL

Scallops with Dill

INGREDIENTS:

12 scallops
2oz butter
2 small leeks, cut into julienne
2 small carrots, cut into julienne
1 courgette, cut into fine batons
$^1/_4$pt dry white wine
2 $^1/_2$ fl.oz. double cream
$^1/_4$ pt fish stock
sea salt & freshly ground white pepper
2 tablespoons chopped dill

To garnish:
Mangetouts, cut into julienne, or sprigs
of dill.

METHOD:

Remove the scallops from their shells. Reserve their liquor. Separate the corals and cut the bodies in half horizontally. Heat half the butter in a large pan, add the vegetables and cook, covered, over a low heat for about 4 minutes, shaking the pan occasionally. Do not allow them to brown. Stir in the stock, scallop liquor, and wine and bring to the boil. Reduce to about 2 $^1/_2$fl.oz, then stir in the cream and simmer for a few minutes until the sauce thickens slightly. Heat the remaining butter, add the scallops, a little salt and most of the dill. Cook gently for 1 minute, turn them over, add corals and cook for a further minute – do not allow them to brown or toughen.

Tip a little of the scallop cooking liquor into the sauce and stir briefly to mix.

Meanwhile blanche, refresh and drain the julienne of mangetouts if using. Divide the sauce and vegetables between 4 warmed dishes and arrange the scallops and corals on top. Sprinkle with the remaining dill and garnish with julienne of mangetouts or sprigs of dill

Noisettes of Lamb with Tarragon

TRIDENT HOTEL

INGREDIENTS:

3 tablespoons Walnut oil
50g/2oz butter
12 noisettes of lamb,seasoned
6 tablespoons Sercial Madeira (dry
sherry will substitute)
2 tablespoons Tarragon,coarsely
chopped
4 tablespoons double cream
Salt & freshly ground black pepper

To garnish:
Tarragon leaves.

METHOD:

In a sauteuse or large frying pan heat the oil and half the butter. Add the noisettes and cook for about 3 minutes on each side or until they are pink in the centre and still moist. Remove with a slotted spoon,cover and keep warm. Tip off the excess oil from the pan,then melt the remaining butter in it. Stir in the madeira,dislodging the sediment,then stir in the Tarragon and cream. Boil until slightly thickened,then pass through a sieve. Season and divide between 4 warmed plates. Place 3 noisettes on each plate and garnish with Tarragon leaves.

TRIDENT HOTEL

Orange & Strawberry Surprise

INGREDIENTS:

4 large oranges
1 pint vanilla ice cream
2 tablespoons Grand Marnier
1 tablespoon brandy
8oz strawberries

METHOD:

Slice the tops of the oranges and remove the flesh. Seed and liquidize the orange flesh. Dice the strawberries. Blend the liquidized oranges and strawberries,ice-cream,brandy,and Grand Marnier. Replace in empty orange shells. Replace top and freeze.Remove from freezer 15 minutes prior to serving.

Cointreau & Chocolate Mousse

INGREDIENTS:

6 eggs
4oz chocolate
$^{1}/_{2}$ pint whipped cream
2 tablespoons Cointreau

METHOD:

Separate egg whites from yolks
Whip the egg whites to a light foam. Melt chocolate. Add the Cointreau to the egg yolks and 3oz of the chocolate. Fold the egg whites into the mixture. Pipe into a glass. Decorate with whipped cream and grated chocolate.

The Vintage

Smoked trout mousse
Baked Irish brie

Cream of celeriac soup
Fresh tomato & orange soup

Garlic spinach
Baked stuffed courgettes

Warm salad of spinach & duck liver
Cucumber salad my way

Turbot in filo pastry
Escalope of salmon with tarragon sauce

Brace of quail stuffed with game mousse

Almond tulip with ice-cream & fruit
Strawberry ice-cream
Hot love

Smoked Trout Mousse

THE VINTAGE

INGREDIENTS:

1 ¹/₂ lbs. smoked trout (fillets, no bones)
3 oz. parsley
1 medium onion
1 dill cucumber
2 tsp. dry dill
4 oz. mayonnaise
 Juice of 1 lemon
6 gelatine leaves
4 egg whites
 Salt and pepper to taste

METHOD:

Combine the first 5 ingredients into a food processor until very fine. Add the lemon juice, melted gelatine and mayonnaise. Beat the egg whites stiff and fold in. Taste for seasoning. Refrigerate until set – 2 to 3 hours.

Baked Irish Brie

INGREDIENTS:

1 ¹/₂ lb. Irish Brie
1 lb. white breadcrumbs
5 eggs (beaten)
 Flour
 Salt and pepper
 Parsley

METHOD:

Cut the Brie in 8 equal pieces and sprinkle with salt and pepper. Roll in flour, then the egg, then breadcrumbs then the egg again and then breadcrumbs again. Make sure the corners are well coated. Bake in hot fat (deep fat fryer) until nicely coloured.
Serve with cranberry sauce and fried parsley.

Cream of Celeriac

THE VINTAGE

INGREDIENTS:

2 lb. celeriac (cleaned and peeled)
shredded)
$^1/_4$ pt. cream
1 oz. flour
2 pt. chicken stock
1 onion (diced)
5 tbsp. oil for cooking
  Nutmeg, pepper and salt.

METHOD:

Sauté onion in oil, add the flour to make a roux. Add the chicken stock and bring to the boil. Add the shredded celeriac and boil for 25 minutes. Taste with nutmeg, pepper and salt. Purée the soup in liquidiser. Bring back to the boil and add cream. Taste for seasoning.

Fresh Tomato and Orange Soup

INGREDIENTS:

2 lb. tomatoes (very ripe)
2 oz. flour
2 onions (diced)
6 smoked back rashers (with rind) diced
3 oranges
$^1/_2$ celery (diced)
1 carrot (diced)
2 pt. chicken stock
10 black peppercorns
2 bay leaves (large)
  Sugar
  Vinegar
  Salt
  Oil for cooking.

METHOD:

Sauté the rashers, onions, celery, carrot, black peppercorns and bay leaves for 8-10 minutes without colouring.
Sprinkle the flour and add the chicken stock. Bring back to the boil. Add the tomatoes and oranges (cut in quarters with peel) and simmer for 25 minutes. Taste with sugar, vinegar and salt. Strain the soup and serve hot with a little whipped cream and orange zest (rind of an orange very finely cut into strips and cooked in water and sugar).

95

Garlic Spinach

THE VINTAGE

INGREDIENTS:

2 oz. butter
2 cloves
2 tsp. lemon juice
2 lb. spinach
$^{1}/_{4}$ pt. cream
  Salt and pepper.

METHOD:

Melt the butter. Add crushed garlic and lemon juice. Wash the spinach carefully discarding the stalks. Shake dry and add to butter. Cook gently for 8-10 minutes, turning constantly. Remove from pan and chop finely. Stir in the cream and seasoning. Heat thoroughly in a clean saucepan.

Baked Stuffed Courgettes

INGREDIENTS:

4 medium size courgettes.

STUFFING:

1 lb. white bread
1 lb. butter
12 garlic cloves
1 medium onion (diced)
  Parsley

METHOD

Half the courgettes and hollow them with an apple corer.
Put the bread, garlic and parsley in a liquidiser and mince finely.
Saute onion in butter and add the breadcrumbs. Add the salt and pepper to taste and cook for one minute, stirring constanyly.
Stuff the mixture into the hollowed courgettes.
Bake the courgettes in oven 400F. Gas 6, 200C for 10 minutes.

Cucumber Salad - My Way

THE VINTAGE

INGREDIENTS:

2 medium cucumbers (thinly sliced)
1 onion (diced)
1 tbsp. dill, finely chopped
4 oz. vinegar
2 tbsp. sugar
$^1/_2$ tbsp. salt
  Ground black pepper
2 tbsp. vegetable oil.

METHOD:

Combine all ingredients and put the sliced cucumber into this mixture
Allow to stand for 2 hours in the fridge

Warm Salad of Spinach and Duck Liver

INGREDIENTS:

8 pieces of duck liver
4 smoked back rashers
$^1/_2$ small onion
1 lb. spinach
  Salt and Pepper
  Garlic
  Nutmeg
2 tbsp. butter.

METHOD:

Sauté liver for 1 minute. Take out of pan and keep warm. In the same
pan put diced onions and rashers. Sauté but do not brown.
Blanch spinach. Toss spinach, garlic and nutmeg in butter.
Arrange spinach on plate with warm liver on top.
Garnish with bread croûtons.

Turbot in Filo Pastry

THE VINTAGE

NGREDIENTS:

16 medium sheets of filo pastry (bought
in store)
24 oz. of Turbot fillet (skinned and diced
to 1ins. squares)
2 medium sized leeks (washed and
roughly chopped)
1 onion diced
1 lb. butter melted
  Salt, white pepper, lemon juice.

METHOD:

Season fish with pepper, lemon juice and salt. Steam for 1-1$\frac{1}{2}$ minutes. Sauté onions and leeks until tender (but not brown) in a little butter. Brush the filo pastry sheets on both sides with melted butter and put 4 sheets for every parcel on top of each other with one tablespoon of leeks and $\frac{1}{4}$ of fish cubes.

Take the opposite corners and fold the parcel. Pinch with thumb and forefinger to keep together.

Bake in the oven 375F 190C Gas 5 for 20-25 minutes or until golden brown.

Escalope of Salmon with Tarragon Sauce

INGREDIENTS:

7 oz. salmon thinly cut
2 shallots
2 oz. cream
2 oz. butter
1 oz. white wine
1 oz. wine vinegar
  Salt and Pepper and Tarragon

METHOD:

Poach the salmon with the shallots, white wine and vinegar. Remove the salmon once it is cooked. Add cream and reduce the liquid to $\frac{3}{4}$. Add the butter and tarragon - do not allow to boil. Pour the sauce around the salmon.

Garnish with cress and lemon.

Brace of Quail
Stuffed with a Game Mousse

THE VINTAGE

INGREDIENTS:

8 quail, deboned
1 lb. lean venison
³/4 pt. of cream
3 egg whites
Salt and pepper
3 tsp. ground green cardamom.
Sauce:
1 pt. of game stock.
Juice of 3 oranges
3 sherry glasses of port wine
(reduce all the above to ¹/4 quantity)
Taste for salt. Maybe add a little more
Port and orange juice.

METHOD:

Game Mousse:
Mince venison very fine or put through food processor. Add egg whites, salt and pepper and cardamom. Keep cool. Add cream. Taste for seasoning.
Fill the deboned quail with mousse, to the original shape and fry in a little butter, then place in a hot oven for 12-14 minutes at 450F 230C Gas 8.

THE VINTAGE

Hot Love

(hot raspberries with vanilla ice cream flamed with Framboise)

ICE CREAM
1 pt. milk.
^{1}/2 pt. cream
8 oz. sugar
8 large egg yolks

1 vanilla pod.
1 lb. raspberries
^{1}/2 pt. water
  Sugar to taste
  Lemon Juice to taste
^{1}/2 tbsp. cornflour.
Framboise (raspberry Schnapps)

METHOD
Take the milk, cream, sugar and vanilla pod (halved lengthwise) and bring to the boil. Let stand for 10 minutes. Take a little of the hot milk and beat in the 8 egg yolks, bring back to the heat until the custard coats the back of a spoon (do not let it boil). Freeze in the ice cream machine, or freezer compartment of 'fridge

HOT RASPBERRIES:
Boil the water, sugar, lemon juice and thicken with cornflour. Add the raspberries. Put the hot raspberries into a serving dish, pour a measure of Raspberry Schnapps on to it and flambé. While it is burning add two scoops of vanilla ice cream.

Almond Tulip with Ice Cream and Fruit

INGREDIENTS:
PASTRY
4 oz. flour
4 oz. icing sugar
3 eggs.
STRAWBERRY ICE CREAM
INGREDIENTS:
1^1/2lbs. strawberries when defrosted or fresh without juice.
1 litre liduid (water and strawberry juice from frozen fruit, if used)
14 oz. sugar
7 oz. glucose
  Juice of 1 lemon
1 egg white.

METHOD:

Make a batter from all the ingredients. Let stand for 2 hours. Pre-heat oven to 400F 200C Gas 6. Place baking paper on a non stick baking tray. Place 1 tbsp. of batter on baking tray very evenly and thinly. Bake in oven for 4-6 minutes. Remove from oven and take the tulip off baking paper immediately. Fold over a glass jar to get the shape. Work very fast otherwise the pastry will go hard.

METHOD:
Liquidise the strawberries. Combine all other ingredients.
Freeze in an ice-cream machine or freezer compartment of 'fridge.

The White House

Feulletés de saumon Florentine

Tomato soup
Crème Vichysoisse

Florida salad
Monte Cristo salad

Seafood layers with red pepper sauce

Chef's special steak
Stuffed breast of veal
Chicken milady

Crème Caramel
Bailey's chilled soufflé

THE WHITE HOUSE

Feuilletés de Saumon Florentine

INGREDIENTS:

12oz. salmon
14 oz. puff pastry
  Butter
  Chopped fresh dill
3 medium sized potatoes
16 large spinach leaves
  Salt and pepper

SAUCE INGREDIENTS:

$1/_8$ pt. of white wine
$1/_4$ pt. cream
  Tarragon
  Parsley
$1/_8$ pt. fish stock
8oz butter
  Dill
  Chives

METHOD:

Peel the potatoes and boil until nearly cooked but still firm. Line 4 buttered feuilleté moulds with puff pastry overlapping the edges. Place 4 leaves of blanched spinach into each mould and allow to overlap. Dice the salmon and potatoes and fry in hot butter until lightly brown. Add the chopped dill and season well. Fill the inside of each case and fold over the spinach. Place a little round of puff pastry on top of each case. Lightly egg wash and fold over the overlapping puff pastry. Place in a moderate oven until golden brown (approx 20 minutes). Turn out onto a plate and surround with a herb butter sauce.

METHOD:

Pour the white wine into a heavy saucepan and reduce to a glaze. Pour in the fish stock and reduce to a glaze again. Add the chopped fresh herbs and cream and reduce until thick. Cut the butter into small cubes and add them gradually over a very low heat until all the butter has emulsified into the sauce.
Garnish with cooked mussels in half shells.

Tomato Soup

THE WHITE HOUSE

INGREDIENTS:

2 pt. chicken stock
1 oz. bacon rind
2 oz. carrots
2 oz. onions
1 $\frac{1}{2}$ lb. tomatoes
2 oz. flour
2 oz. butter
1 dessertspoon sugar
2 dessertspoons tomato puree
 Salt and pepper

METHOD:

Fry onion and bacon rind in the butter until lightly brown. Add carrots and fry a little. Add the flour and cook for 1 minute. Add tomatoes and chicken stock gradually. Bring to the boil and skim. Add the sugar and simmer for 1 hour. Pass through a blender and strain. Add seasoning to taste.

Crème Vichyssoise

INGREDIENTS:

3 leeks diced
2 oz. onion finely diced
1 oz. chives finely chopped
9 oz. potatoes diced
1 oz. butter
1 $\frac{3}{4}$ pt. chicken stock
Salt, Cayenne pepper
$\frac{1}{4}$ pt. cream

METHOD:

Sweat the onions, potatoes and leeks in butter until soft but not brown. Add the stock and simmer until potatoes are soft. Season and pass through a fine sieve. Chill in the fridge. Serve with a little whipped cream on top and chopped chives as a garnish.

THE WHITE HOUSE

Florida Salad

INGREDIENTS:

1 lettuce
2 large oranges
$^1/_2$ pt. acidulated cream ($^1/_2$ pt. cream, juice of a lemon)

METHOD:

Remove the orange zest with a peeler. Cut into very fine strips. Put the strips into boiling water for a few seconds and refresh under cold water. Peel the oranges removing all the white skin. Cut the segment clear of skin and remove pips. Arrange the lettuce decoratively in 4 bowls and arrange the orange segments on the lettuce. Pour the acidulated cream over the salad (orange juice and caster sugar may be added to the cream). Sprinkle with the orange zest.

Monte Cristo Salad

INGREDIENTS:

1 medium sized lobster cooked
2 small potatoes cooked
1 medium truffle
1 hard boiled egg
2 heads of lettuce

METHOD:

Dice the lobster meat and the potatoes and mix together with sliced truffle and hard boiled egg, sliced. Bind with some mayonnaise. Arrange the lettuce in a serving dish and place the salad on top. Serve chilled.

Seafood Layers
with Red Pepper Sauce

THE WHITE HOUSE

INGREDIENTS:

8 fillets of plaice
8oz. raw salmon
8oz. fresh cream
1 egg white
  Lemon juice
4oz. very fine breadcrumbs
  Seasoning.

SAUCE:

4 skinned red peppers
$^1/_4$ pt. chicken stock
1 clove of garlic
  Cream
  Seasoning

METHOD:

Mince the salmon very finely. Place the salmon in a mixer and gradually add the egg white, lemon juice, cream and seasoning. Place some salmon mousse between each fillet of plaice in layers in a ceramic dish. Add a little white wine. Cover with tin foil and bake in a moderate oven until cooked, approximately 10 minutes. Put onto a plate. Lightly sprinkle with breadcrumbs and place under a hot grill until golden brown. Surround with sauce and garnish with mussels in half shell and diced chives.

METHOD:

Boil the peppers, garlic and chicken stock until peppers are soft. Place in liquidiser. Add a little cream and seasoning. Return to heat and reduce to sauce consistency.

Chef's Special

THE WHITE HOUSE

INGREDIENTS:

8   6 oz. fillet steaks.
2 oz. butter
  Seasoning

SAUCE NUMBER 1.

$^1/_2$ onion
1 oz. butter
4 tomatoes
  Seasoning

SAUCE NUMBER 2

$^1/_2$ onion
1 oz. butter
2 oz. button mushrooms sliced
2 tomatoes
2 oz. tomato purée
1 pt. demi glace
Measure whiskey
  Seasoning

METHOD:
Batten fillet steaks into medallion shapes. Fry in the butter until cooked to taste. Place sauce number one between two medallions and cover with sauce number two.

METHOD:

Fry the onions, finely chopped, in the butter until golden. Add the chopped tomatoes and simmer for 10 minutes. Add seasoning.

METHOD:

Fry the onions in butter until golden. Add the sliced mushrooms and brown lightly. Add whiskey and flambé. Stir in the tomato purée and add demi glace*. Add chopped tomatoes and simmer for 40 minutes. Season to taste.

*For demi-glace see P. 7

Chicken Milady

THE WHITE HOUSE

INGREDIENTS:

4 chicken breasts
$^1/_4$ pt. white wine
$^3/_4$ pt. cream
$^1/_2$ red pepper
$^1/_2$ green pepper
$^1/_2$ small onion
$^1/_4$ pt. chicken stock
  Butter
  Seasoning

METHOD:

Melt a knob of butter in a large frying pan. Lightly fry the breasts of chicken without colouring. Add the finely diced onion and peppers and fry gently without browning. Add the white wine and reduce by half. Add the chicken stock and reduce by half. Pour in the cream and gently simmer until the sauce is of coating consistency. Season to taste. Serve the chicken on a bed of brown rice with seasonal fruits or julienne of red and green peppers and orange and lemon zest with perhaps a tomato rose as garnish.

Stuffed Breast of Veal

INGREDIENTS:

2 lbs. of veal breast

STUFFING:

8oz. fine sausage meat
$^1/_4$ of a small onion finely chopped
  Grated zest of $^1/_2$ a lemon
1 small egg
  Tarragon and Chives.
6 chopped mushrooms
  Chopped parsley
  Seasoning.

METHOD:

STUFFING:
To make the stuffing first fry the onions and mushrooms in butter until light brown. Then add the rest of the ingredients. Cut open the thickest part of the veal breast to form a pocket. Place the stuffing in the pocket and seal either using cocktail sticks or by stitching. Place the meat in a braising pan on a bed of chopped vegetables. Half cover the joint with veal stock and place in a moderate oven with a tight lid for approximately 3 hours. Serve the reduced cooking liquor as a sauce.

THE WHITE HOUSE

Crème Caramel

INGREDIENTS:

2 oz. sugar
1 oz. water
$^1\!/_2$ pt. milk
2 oz. sugar
2 eggs
1 vanilla pod

METHOD:

Boil the sugar and water until at caramel stage (lightly brown). Pour into charlotte mould and allow to set. Bring the milk to the boil with the vanilla pod and pour onto the eggs and sugar. Strain and pour over the caramel and place in a bain marie until set. Allow to cool and set. Turn out onto a plate and decorate.

Bailey's Chilled Soufflé

INGREDIENTS:

3 eggs
$^1\!/_2$ pt. cream
4 oz. caster sugar
2 leaves of gelatine
  Double measure of Baileys
  Juice of one lemon

METHOD:

Place the leaves of gelatine in cold water. Separate the egg and put egg yolks into a stainless steel pot with the lemon juice, sugar and Baileys. Whisk over a low heat until light and fluffy. Add the soft gelatine leaves to the mixture and whisk until completely dissolved. Add the lightly whipped cream. Stir in the stiffly whipped egg whites. Pour into moulds and allow to set. To serve turn the soufflés onto plates and surround with pouring cream and decorate appropriately.